600+

New Pattern Case Based MCQs for

CBSE BOARD CLASS 10

Science, Mathematics & Social Studies

Corporate Office

DISHA PUBLICATION

45, 2nd Floor, Maharishi Dayanand Marg,
Corner Market, Malviya Nagar, New Delhi - 110017
Tel : 49842349 / 49842350

Typeset by Disha DTP Team

www.dishapublication.com
Books &
ebooks for
School &
Competitive
Exams

www.mylearninggraph.com
Etests
for
Competitive
Exams

Write to us at **feedback_disha@aiets.co.in**

Contents

Latest Revised Syllabus Issued by CBSE for Academic Year (2020-2021)

COURSE STRUCTURE CLASS X (2020-21)

Time: 3 Hours   (Annual Examination)   **Max. Marks: 80**

Unit No.	Unit	Marks
I	Chemical Substances-Nature and Behaviour	26
II	World of Living	23
III	Natural Phenomena	12
IV	Effects of Current	14
V	Natural Resources	5
	Total	80
	Internal assessment	20
	Grand Total	100

Theme: Materials

Unit I: Chemical Substances - Nature and Behaviour

Chemical reactions: Chemical equation, Balanced chemical equation, implications of a balanced chemical equation, types of chemical reactions: combination, decomposition, displacement, double displacement, precipitation, neutralization, oxidation and reduction.

Acids, bases and salts: Their definitions in terms of furnishing of H^+ and OH^- ions, General properties, examples and uses, concept of pH scale (Definition relating to logarithm not required), importance of pH in everyday life; preparation and uses of Sodium Hydroxide, Bleaching powder, Baking soda, Washing soda and Plaster of Paris.

Metals and nonmetals: Properties of metals and non-metals; Reactivity series; Formation and properties of ionic compounds;

✘	**Basic metallurgical processes; Corrosion and its prevention.**

Carbon compounds: Covalent bonding in carbon compounds, Versatile nature of carbon, Homologous series.

✘	**Nomenclature of carbon compounds containing functional groups (halogens, alcohol, ketones, aldehydes, alkanes and alkynes), difference between saturated hydrocarbons and unsaturated hydrocarbons. Chemical properties of carbon compounds (combustion, oxidation, addition and substitution reaction). Ethanol and Ethanoic acid (only properties and uses), soaps and detergents.**

Periodic classification of elements: Need for classification, early attempts at classification of elements (Dobereiner's Triads, Newland's Law of Octaves, Mendeleev's Periodic Table), Modern periodic table, gradation in properties, valency, atomic number, metallic and non-metallic properties.

Theme: The World of the Living

Unit II : World of Living

Life processes: 'Living Being'. Basic concept of nutrition, respiration, transport and excretion in plants and animals.

| ✘ | Control and co-ordination in animals and plants: Tropic movements in plants; Introduction of plant hormones; Control and co-ordination in animals: Nervous system; Voluntary, involuntary and reflex action; Chemical co-ordination: animal hormones. |

Reproduction: Reproduction in animals and plants (asexual and sexual) reproductive health-need and methods of family planning. Safe sex vs HIV/AIDS. Child bearing and women's health.

Heredity and Evolution: Heredity; Mendel's contribution- Laws for inheritance of traits: Sex determination: brief introduction;

| ✘ | Basic concepts of evolution |

Theme: Natural Phenomena

Unit III : Natural Phenomena

Reflection of light by curved surfaces; Images formed by spherical mirrors, centre of curvature, principal axis, principal focus, focal length, mirror formula (Derivation not required), magnification.

Refraction; Laws of refraction, refractive index.

Refraction of light by spherical lens; Image formed by spherical lenses; Lens formula (Derivation not required); Magnification. Power of a lens.

| ✘ | Functioning of a lens in human eye, defects of vision and their corrections, applications of spherical mirrors and lenses. |

Refraction of light through a prism, dispersion of light, scattering of light, applications in daily life.

Theme: How Things Work

Unit IV : Effects of Current

Electric current, potential difference and electric current. Ohm's law; Resistance, Resistivity, Factors on which the resistance of a conductor depends. Series combination of resistors, parallel combination of resistors and its applications in daily life. Heating effect of electric current and its applications in daily life. Electric power, Interrelation between P, V, I and R.

Magnetic effects of current : Magnetic field, field lines, field due to a current carrying conductor, field due to current carrying coil or solenoid; Force on current carrying conductor, Fleming's Left Hand Rule, Electric Motor, Electromagnetic induction. Induced potential difference, Induced current. Fleming's Right Hand Rule,

| ✘ | Electric Generator, Direct current. Alternating current: frequency of AC. Advantage of AC over DC. Domestic electric circuits. |

Theme: Natural Resources

Unit V: Natural Resources

| ✘ | Sources of energy: Different forms of energy, conventional and non-conventional sources of energy: Fossil fuels, solar energy; biogas; wind, water and tidal energy; Nuclear energy. Renewable versus non-renewable sources of Energy. |

Our environment: Eco-system, Environmental problems, Ozone depletion, waste production and their solutions.

Biodegradable and non-biodegradable substances.

| ✘ | Management of natural resources: Conservation and judicious use of natural resources. Forest and wild life; Coal and Petroleum conservation. Examples of people's participation for conservation of natural resources. Big dams: advantages and limitations; alternatives, if any. Water harvesting. Sustainability of natural resources. |

Note: *Topics/Chapters/Units in the boxes are not in the syllabus for the academic year 2020-21.*

SCIENCE
Case Study Based MCQs

<u>CBSE Sample Paper 2021</u>

INSTRUCTION: Question 1 to 44 are case based questions. Attempt any 4 sub parts. Each question carry 1 mark.

1. **Read the following and answer any four questions from 1 (i) to 1 (v).**

   All living cells require energy for various activities. This energy is available by the breakdown of simple carbohydrates either using oxygen or without using oxygen.

   (i) Energy in the case of higher plants and animals is obtained by

      (a) Breathing   b) Tissue respiration

      (c) Organ respiration   (d) Digestion of food

   (ii) The graph below represents the blood lactic acid concentration of an athlete during a race of 400 m and shows a peak at point D.

   Lactic acid production has occurred in the athlete while running in the 400 m race.

   Respiration in athletics

   The blood of an athlete was tested before, during and after a 400m race:

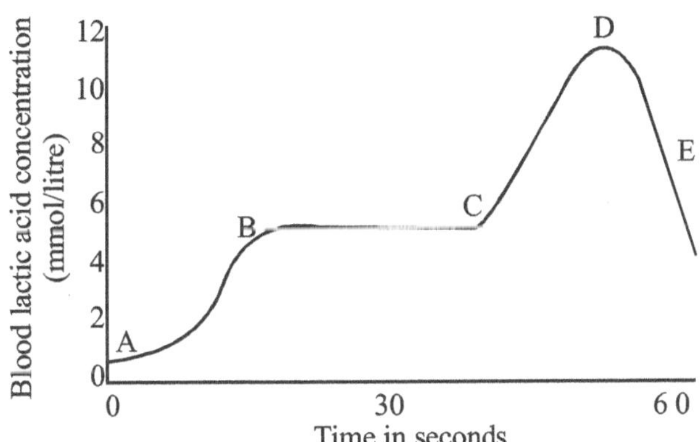

   Lactic acid production has occurred in the athlete while running in the 400 m race. Which of the following processes explains this event?

   Which of the following processes explains this event?

      (a) Aerobic respiration   (b) Anaerobic respiration

      (c) Fermentation   (d) Breathing

(iii) Study the graph below that represents the amount of energy supplied with respect to the time while an athlete is running at full speed.

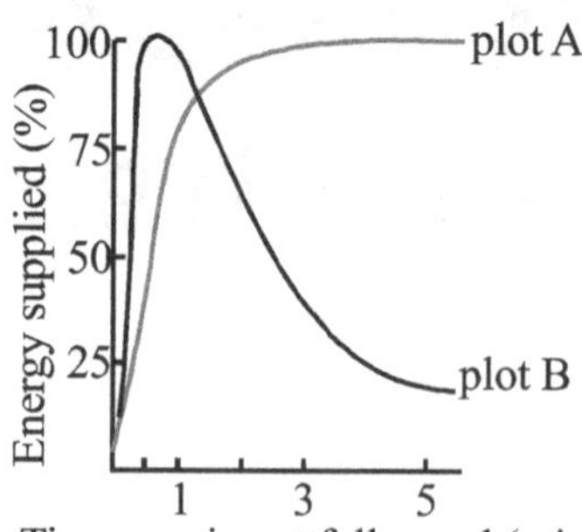

Choose the correct combination of plots and justification provided in the following table.

Plot A	Plot B	Justification
(a) Aerobic	Anaerobic	Amount of energy is low and inconsistent in aerobic and high in anaerobic
(b) Aerobic	Anaerobic	Amount of energy is high and consistent in aerobic and low in anaerobic
(c) Anaerobic	Aerobic	Amount of energy is high and consistent in aerobic and low in anaerobic
(d) Anaerobic	Aerobic	Amount of energy is high and inconsistent in anaerobic and low in aerobic

(iv) The characteristic processes observed in anaerobic respiration are:

    (i)   presence of oxygen

    (ii)   release of carbon dioxide

    (iii) release of energy

    (iv) release of lactic acid

    (a)   (i), (ii) only

    (b)   (i), (ii), (iii) only

    (c)   (ii), iii), iv) only

    (d)   (iv) only

(v) Study the table below and select the row that has the incorrect information.

		Aerobic	Anaerobic
(a)	**Location**	Cytoplasm	Mitochondria
(b)	**End Porduct**	CO_2 and H_2O	Ethanol and CO_2
(c)	**Amount of ATP**	High	Low
(d)	**Oxygen**	Needed	Not needed

2. **Read the following and answer any four questions from (i) to (v).**

Metallic Character The ability of an atom to donate electrons and form positive ion (cation) is known as electropositivity or metallic character. Down the group, metallic character increases due to increase in atomic size and across the period, from left to right electropositivity decreases due to decrease in atomic size. Non-Metallic Character The ability of an atom to accept electrons to form a negative ion (anion) is called non-metallic character or electronegativity. The elements having high electro-negativity have a higher tendency to gain electrons and form anion. Down the group, electronegativity decreases due to increase in atomic size and across the period, from left to right electronegativity increases due to decrease in atomic size.

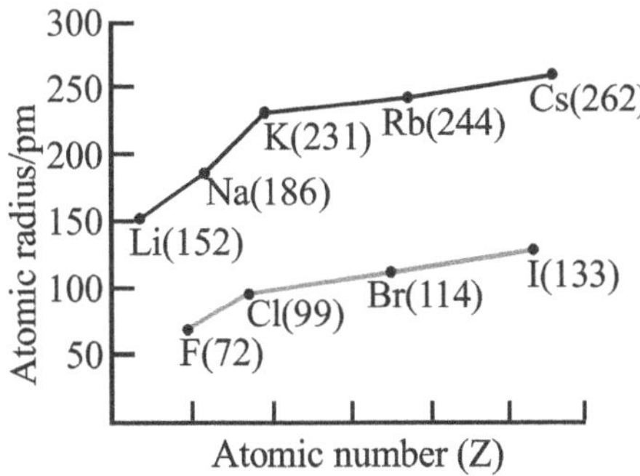

(i) Which of the following correctly represents the decreasing order of metallic character of Alkali metals plotted in the graph?

(a) $Cs > Rb > Li > Na > K$ (b) $K > Rb > Li > Na > Cs$

(c) $Cs > Rb > K > Na > Li$ (d) $Cs > K > Rb > Na > Li$

(ii) Hydrogen is placed along with Alkali metals in the modern periodic table though it shows non-metallic character

(a) as Hydrogen has one electron & readily loses electron to form negative ion

(b) as Hydrogen can easily lose one electron like alkali metals to form positive ion

(c) as Hydrogen can gain one electron easily like Halogens to form negative ion

(d) as Hydrogen shows the properties of non-metals

(iii) Which of the following has highest electronegativity?

(a) F (b) Cl (c) Br (d) I

(iv) Identify the reason for the gradual change in electronegativity in halogens down the group.

(a) Electronegativity increases down the group due to decrease in atomic size

(b) Electronegativity decreases down the group due to decrease in tendency to lose electrons

(c) Electronegativity decreases down the group due to increase in atomic radius/ tendency to gain electron decreases

(d) Electronegativity increases down the group due to increase in forces of attractions between nucleus & valence electrons

(v) Which of the following reason correctly justifies that "Fluorine (72pm) has smaller atomic radius than Lithium (152pm)"?

    (a) F and Li are in the same group. Atomic size increases down the group

    (b) F and Li are in the same period. Atomic size increases across the period due to increase in number of shells

    (c) F and Li are in the same group. Atomic size decreases down the group

    (d) F and Li are in the same period and across the period atomic size/radius decreases from left to right.

3. **Read the following and answer any four questions from (i) to (v)**

Sumati wanted to see the stars of the night sky. She knows that she needs a telescope to see those distant stars. She finds out that the telescopes, which are made of lenses, are called refracting telescopes and the ones which are made of mirrors are called reflecting telescopes.

Telescope Diagram

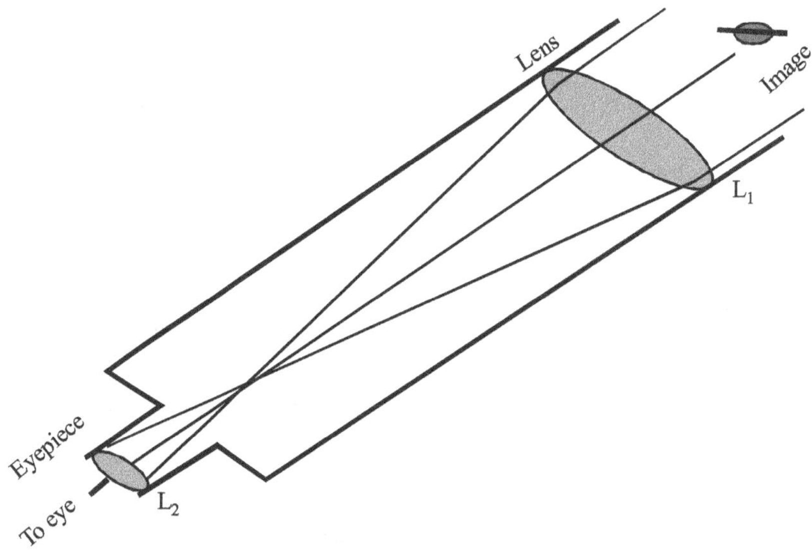

So she decided to make a refracting telescope. She bought two lenses, L_1 and L_2, out of which L_1 was bigger and L_2 was smaller. The larger lens gathers and bends the light, while the smaller lens magnifies the image. Big, thick lenses are more powerful. So to see far away, she needed a big powerful lens. Unfortunately, she realized that a big lens is very heavy. Heavy lenses are hard to make and difficult to hold in the right place. Also, since the light is passing through the lens, the surface of the lens has to be extremely smooth. Any flaws in the lens will change the image. It would be like looking through a dirty window.

(i) Based on the diagram shown, what kind of lenses would Sumati need to make the telescope?

    (a) Concave lenses   (b) Convex lenses

    (c) Bifocal lenses   (d) Flat lenses

(ii) If the powers of the lenses L_1 and L_2 are in the ratio of 4:1, what would be the ratio of the focal length of L_1 and L_2?

    (a) 4 : 1   (b) 1 : 4   (c) 2 : 1   (d) 1 : 1

(iii) What is the formula for magnification obtained with a lens?

    (a) Ratio of height of image to height of object

    (b) Double the focal length.

    (c) Inverse of the radius of curvature.

    (d) Inverse of the object distance.

(iv) Sumati did some preliminary experiment with the lenses and found out that the magnification of the eyepiece (L_2) is 3. If in her experiment with L_2 she found an image at 24 cm from the lens, at what distance did she put the object?

    (a) 72 cm   (b) 12 cm   (c) 8 cm   (d) 6 cm

(v) Sumati bought not-so-thick lenses for the telescope and polished them. What advantages, if any, would she have with her choice of lenses?

    (a) She will not have any advantage as even thicker lenses would give clearer images.

    (b) Thicker lenses would have made the telescope easier to handle.

    (c) Not-so-thick lenses would not make the telescope very heavy and also allow considerable amount of light to pass.

    (d) Not-so-thick lenses will give her more magnification.

4. **Read the following and answer any 4 questions from (i) to (v).**

A solenoid is a long helical coil of wire through which a current is run in order to create a magnetic field. The magnetic field of the solenoid is the superposition of the fields due to the current through each coil. It is nearly uniform inside the solenoid and close to zero outside and is similar to the field of a bar magnet having a north pole at one end and a south pole at the other depending upon the direction of current flow. The magnetic field produced in the solenoid is dependent on a few factors such as, the current in the coil, number of turns per unit length etc. The following graph is obtained by a researcher while doing an experiment to see the variation of the magnetic field with respect to the current in the solenoid. The unit of magnetic field as given in the graph attached is in milli-Tesla (mT) and the current is given in Ampere.

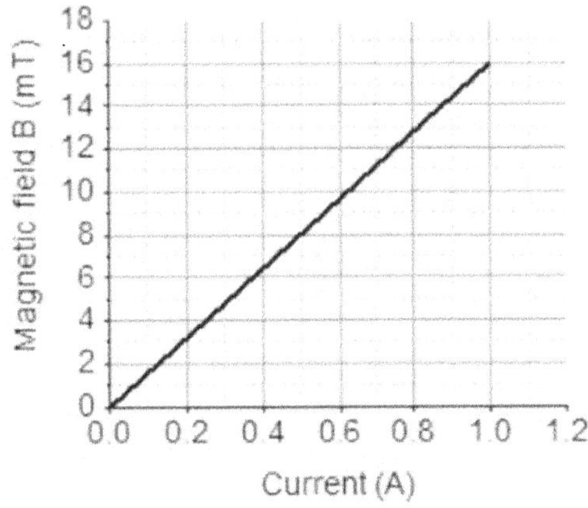

(i) What type of energy conversion is observed in a linear solenoid?

    (a) Mechanical to Magnetic   (b) Electrical to Magnetic

    (c) Electrical to Mechanical   (d) Magnetic to Mechanical

(ii) What will happen if a soft iron bar is placed inside the solenoid?

    (a) The bar will be electrocuted resulting in short-circuit.

    (b) The bar will be magnetised as long as there is current in the circuit.

    (c) The bar will be magnetised permanently.

    (d) The bar will not be affected by any means.

(iii) The magnetic field lines produced inside the solenoid are similar to that of …

    (a) a bar magnet 10   (b) a straight current carrying conductor

    (c) a circular current carrying loop   (d) electromagnet of any shape

(iv) After analysing the graph a student writes the following statements.

    I.   The magnetic field produced by the solenoid is inversely proportional to the current.

    II. The magnetic field produced by the solenoid is directly proportional to the current.

    III. The magnetic field produced by the solenoid is directly proportional to square of the current.

    IV. The magnetic field produced by the solenoid is independent of the current.

    Choose from the following which of the following would be the correct statement(s).

    (a) Only IV   (b) I and III and IV   (c) I and II   (d) Only II

(v) From the graph deduce which of the following statements is correct.

    (a) For a current of 0.8A the magnetic field is 13 mT

    (b) For larger currents, the magnetic field increases non-linearly.

    (c) For a current of 0.8A the magnetic field is 1.3 mT

    (d) There is not enough information to find the magnetic field corresponding to 0.8A current.

Practice Case Study MCQs

Directions: Q. No. 5-8 contain five sub-parts each. You are expected to answer **any four** sub-parts in these questions.

5.   **Read the following and answer any four questions from 5 (i) to 5 (v)**

Most carbon compounds are poor conductors of electricity. From the data on the boiling and melting points of the above compounds, we can conclude that the forces of attraction between these molecules are not very strong.

Compound	Melting point (K)	Boiling point (K)
Acetic acid (CH_3COOH)	290	391
Chloroform ($CHCl_3$)	209	334
Ethanol (CH_3CH_2OH)	156	351
Methane (CH_4)	90	111

  (i) Generally carbon compounds are

     (a) Covalent compounds   (b) Ionic compounds

     (c) Metallic compounds   (d) Non-stoichiometric compounds

  (ii) Boiling point and melting points of carbon compounds are

     (a) Greater than ionic compounds   (b) Lesser than ionic compounds

     (c) Same as ionic compounds   (d) Insufficient data

  (iii) Glacial acetic acid is

     (a) Pure acetic acid   (b) Solid acetic acid

     (c) Gaseous acetic acid   (d) Frozen acetic acid

  (iv) Graphite is a good conductor of electricity due to presence of

     (a) Deficiency of electron   (b) Presence of free electron

     (c) Presence of free proton   (d) Ionic bonding

  (v) covalent bond is

     (a) Stronger than ionic bond   (b) Weaker than ionic bond

     (c) Same as ionic bond   (d) None of these

6. **Read the following and attempt any four questions from 6 (i) to 6 (v).**

Most human chromosomes have a maternal and a paternal copy, and we have 22 such pairs. But one pair, called the sex chromosomes, is odd in not always being a perfect pair. Women have a perfect pair of sex chromosomes, both called X. But men have a mismatched pair in which one is a normal-sized X while the other is a short one called Y. So women are XX, while men are XY.

  (i) If a normal cell of human body contains 46 pairs of chromosomes then the numbers of chromosomes in a sex cell of a human being is most likely to be:

     (a) 60   (b) 23   (c) 22   (d) 40

  (ii) Which of the following determines the sex of a child?

     (a) The length of the mother's pregnancy

     (b) The length of time between ovulation and copulation

     (c) The presence of an X chromosome in an ovum

     (d) The presence of a Y chromosome in a sperm

  (iii) In human males, all the chromosomes are paired perfectly except one. These unpaired chromosomes are:

     (a) Large chromosome   (b) Small chromosome

     (c) Y chromosome   (d) X chromosome

  (iv) The process where characteristics are transmitted from parent to offsprings is called:

     (a) Variation   (b) Heredity   (c) Gene   (d) Allele

     (e) None of the above

(v) Who have a perfect pair of sex chromosomes?

    (a) Girls only   (b) Boys only

    (c) Both girls and boys   (d) It depends on many other factors

7. **Read the following and answer any four questions from 7(i) to 7(v).**

Light travels through a vacuum at a speed $c = 3 \times 10^8$ m/s. It can also travel through many materials, such as air, water and glass. Atoms in the material absorb, reemit and scatter the light, however. Therefore, light travels through the material at a speed that is less than c, the actual speed depending on the nature of the material. To describe the extent to which the speed of light in a material medium differs from that in a vacuum, we use a parameter called the index of refraction (or refractive index).

(i) Figure shows a ray of light as it travels from medium A to medium B. Retractive index of the medium B relative to medium A is

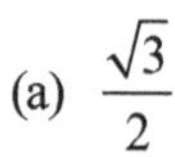

    (a) $\dfrac{\sqrt{3}}{2}$ (b) $\dfrac{\sqrt{2}}{\sqrt{3}}$

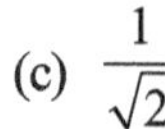

    (c) $\dfrac{1}{\sqrt{2}}$ (d) $\sqrt{2}$

(ii) A light ray enters from medium A to medium B as shown in the figure. The refractive index of medium B relative to A will be

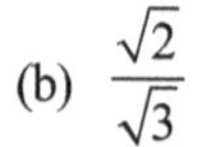
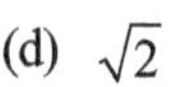

    (a) greater than unity

    (b) less than unity

    (c) equal to unity

    (d) zero

(iii) The path of a ray of light coming from air passing through a rectangular glass slab traced by four students shown as A, B, C and D in the figure. Which one of them is correct?

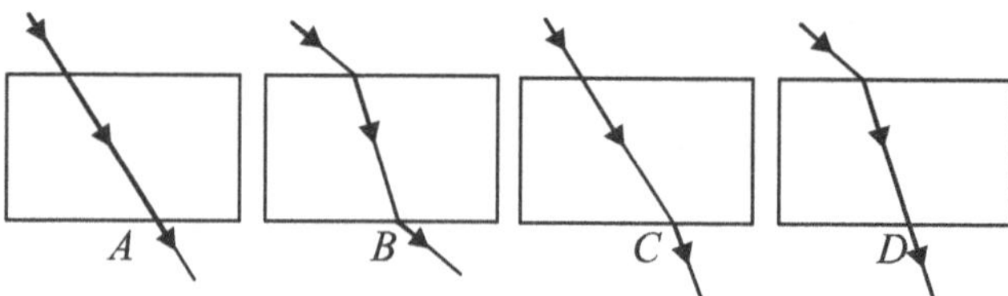

    (a) A (b) B

    (c) C (d) D

(iv) You are given water, mustard oil, glycerine and kerosene. In which of these media, a ray of light incident obliquely at same angle would bend the most?

    (a) Kerosene   (b) Water

    (c) Mustard oil   (d) Glycerine

(v) A ray of light is incident in medium 1 on a surface that separates medium 1 from medium 2. Let v_1 and v_2 represent the velocity of light in medium 1 and medium 2 respectively. Also let n_{12} and n_{21} represent the refractive index of medium 1 with respect to medium 2 and refractive index of medium 2 with respect to medium 1, respectively. If i and r denote the angle of incidence and angle of refraction, then-

(a) $\dfrac{\sin i}{\sin r} = n_{21} = \dfrac{v_1}{v_2}$

(b) $\dfrac{\sin i}{\sin r} = n_{21} = \dfrac{v_2}{v_1}$

(c) $\dfrac{\sin i}{\sin r} = n_{12} = \dfrac{v_1}{v_2}$

(d) $\dfrac{\sin i}{\sin r} = n_{12} = \dfrac{v_2}{v_1}$

8. Read the following and answer any four questions from 8 (i) to 8 (v).

Ozone (O_3) is a molecule formed by three atoms of oxygen. While O_2, which we normally refer to as oxygen, is essential for all arobic forms of life. Ozone is a deadly poison. However, at the higher levels of the atomsphere, ozone performs an essential function. It sheilds the surface of the earth from ultraviolet (UV) radiation from the Sun. This radiation is highly damaging to organisms, for example, it is known to cause skin cancer in human beings. Ozone at the higher levels of the atmosphere is a product of UV radiation acting on oxgen (O_2) molecule. The higher energy UV radiations split apart some moleculer oxygen (O_2) into free oxygen (O) atoms. The amount of ozone in the atmoshphere began to drop sharply in the 1980s. This decrease has been linked to synthetic chemicals like chlorofluorocarbons (CFCs) which are used as refrigerants and in fire extinguishers. In 1987, the United Nations Environment Programme (UNEP) succeeded in forging an agreemennt to freeze CFC production at 1986 levels. It is now mandatory for all the manufacturing companies to make CFC-free referigerators throughout the world.

(i) Ozone molecule is made up of

    (a) 3 oxygen atoms

    (b) 2 oxygen atoms

    (c) 4 oxygen atoms

    (d) 1 oxygen atoms

(ii) Ozone shields the surface of the earth from which radiation?

    (a) IR

    (b) U.V.

    (c) Microwave

    (d) X-ray

(iii) The amount of ozone in the atmosphere began to drop sharply in which decade of the twentieth century?

    (a) 1979

    (b) 1981

    (c) 1980

    (d) None of these

(iv) The United Nations Environment Programme (UNEP) succeeded in forging an agreement to freeze CFC production at which levels?

    (a) 1987

    (b) 1986

    (c) 1980

    (d) 1985

(v) UV radiations are known to cause ______ in humans.

 (a) Skin cancer   (b) Lung cancer

 (c) Asthama   (d) Eye defect

Directions: Q. No. 9-12 contain five sub-parts each. You are expected to answer **any four** sub-parts in these questions.

---

9. **Read the following and answer any four questions from 9 (i) to 9 (v).**

The male reproductive system consists of portions which produce the germ-cells and other portions that deliver the germ-cells to the site of fertilisation. The formation of germ-cells or sperms takes place in the testes. These are located outside the abdominal cavity in scrotum because sperm formation requires a lower temperature than the normal body temperature. We have discussed the role of the testes in the secretion of the hormone, testosterone, in the previous chapter. In addition to regulating the formation of sperms, testosterone brings about changes in appearance seen in boys at the time of puberty. The sperms formed are delivered through the vas deferens which unites with a tube coming from the urinary bladder. The urethra thus forms a common passage for both the sperms and urine. Along the path of the vas deferens, glands like the prostate and the seminal vesicles add their secretions so that the sperms are now in a fluid which makes their transport easier and this fluid also provides nutrition. The sperms are tiny bodies that consist of mainly genetic material and a long tail that helps them to move towards the female germ-cell.

(i) The seminiferous tubules of the testes are lined by the germinal epithelium consisting of

 (a) spermatids   (b) cells of Sertoli

 (c) spermatogonium   (d) spermatocytes

(ii) The seminiferous tubules of the testes are lined by the germinal epithelium consisting of

 (a) sertoli cells   (b) cells of germinal epithelium

 (c) cells of Leydig or interstitial cells (d) secondary spermatocytes

(iii) Another name for Bulbourethral gland is

 (a) Meibomian gland   (b) Prostate gland

 (c) Perineal gland   (d) Cowper's gland

(iv) In man, Cryptorchidism is the condition when

 (a) testes do not descent into the scrotum (b) there are two testes in each scrotum

 (c) testis degenerates in the scrotum (d) testis enlarges in the scrotum

(v) Which of these is an accessory reproductive gland in male mammals

 (a) Inguinal gland   (b) Prostate gland

 (c) Mushroom-shaped gland (d) Gastric gland

10. **Read the following and attempt any four questions from 10(i) to 10(v).**

In many practical applications to have desired value of resistance two or more resistances are required to be combined. This can be done in two ways : in series and in parallel. Sometimes resistances are to be combined in such a way that some resistances be in series and some in parallel. Such a combination is called mixed grouping.

If, in an electrical circuit, two or more resistances connected between two points are replaced by a single resistance such that there is no change in the current of the circuit and in the potential difference between those two points, then the single resistance is called the 'equivalent resistance'. When the resistance of a circuit is to be increased, they are combined in series and when heavy current is to be passed, they are combined in parallel so as to decrease the total resistance.

(i) What is the maximum resistance which can be made using five resistors each of $1/5\ \Omega$?

    (a) $1/5\ \Omega$ (b) $10\ \Omega$ (c) $5\ \Omega$ (d) $1\ \Omega$

(ii) What is the minimum resistance which can be made using five resistors each of $1/5\ \Omega$?

    (a) $1/5\ \Omega$ (b) $1/25\ \Omega$ (c) $1/10\ \Omega$ (d) $25\ \Omega$

(iii) A cylindrical conductor of length l and uniform area of cross-section A has resistance R. Another conductor of length $2l$ and resistance R of the same material has area of cross-section.

    (a) $A/2$ (b) $3A/2$ (c) $2A$ (d) $3A$

(iv) Two resistors of resistance 2Ω and 4Ω when connected to a battery will have

    (a)   same current flowing through them when connected in parallel

    (b)   same current flowing through them when connected in series

    (c)   same potential difference across them when connected in series

    (d)   different potential difference across them when connected in parallel

(v) A piece of wire of resistance R is cut into five equal parts. These parts are then connected in parallel. If the equivalent resistance of this combination is R' then the ratio R/R' is

    (a) $1/25$ (b) $1/5$ (c) 5 (d) 25

11. **Read the following and attempt any four questions from 11(i) to 11(v).**

Question numbers 11(i) – 11(v) are based on the periodic table. Study the part of the modern periodic table presented below in which the alphabets represent the symbols of elements and answer any four questions.

Group → Period ↓	1	12	14	15	16	17
2				M	Q	V
3	A	J			R	W
4	E		L			T
5	G					X

(i) Consult the above part of the periodic table to predict which of the given combination is a covalent compound:

    (a) RQ_2 (b) AT   (c) JQ   (d) JX_2

(ii) Considering the above part of the periodic table, which of the given element is the most electropositive element?

    (a) J   (b) A   (c) G   (d) E

(iii) Which of the given element is the most electronegative element?

    (a) Q   (b) W   (c) X   (d) V

(iv) Which element shows +2 oxidation state?

    (a) A   (b) J   (c) M   (d) V

OR

(v) Which element shows −1 oxidation state in its hydrides.

    (a) A   (b) J   (c) V   (d) Q

12. **Read the following and answer any four questions from 12 (i) to 12 (v).**

The process of digestion in humans is achieved by crushing the food with our teeth. Since the lining of the canal is soft, the food is also wetted to make its passage smooth. When we eat something we like, our mouth 'waters'. This is actually not only water, but a fluid called saliva secreted by the salivary glands. Another aspect of the food we ingest is its complex nature. If it is to be absorbed from the alimentary canal, it has to be broken into smaller molecules. This is done with the help of biological catalysts called enzymes. The saliva contains an enzyme called salivary amylase that breaks down starch which is a complex molecule to give sugar. The food is mixed thoroughly with saliva and moved around the mouth while chewing by the muscular tongue. It is necessary to move the food in a regulated manner along the digestive tube so that it can be processed properly in each part. The lining of canal has muscles that contract rhythmically in order to push the food forward. These peristaltic movements occur all along the gut. From the mouth, the food is taken to the stomach through the food-pipe or oesophagus. The stomach is a large organ which expands when food enters it. The muscular walls of the stomach help in mixing the food thoroughly with more digestive juices. These digestion functions are taken care of by the gastric glands present in the wall of the stomach. These release hydrochloric acid, a protein digesting enzyme called pepsin, and mucus. The hydrochloric acid creates an acidic medium which facilitates the action of the enzyme pepsin. The mucus protects the inner lining of the stomach from the action of the acid under normal conditions.

(i) Doctors will suggest __________ if person is suffering form high blood cholesterol.

    (a) Ghee   (b) Vegetable Oil   (c) Dalda   (d) Lard

(ii) In humans, lacteals are found in __________ .

    (a) Ileum   (b) Oesophagus   (c) Ear   (d) None of the above

(iii) What is the enzyme that breaks down lactose?

    (a) Lipase enzymes   (b) Pepsin

    (c) Amylase   (d) Lactase

(iv) A dental condition that is characterized by hyper mineralization of teeth enamel due to excessive intake of__________ . The teeth often appear mottled.

    (a) Sodium   (b) Calcium   (c) Fluoride   (d) Mercury

(v) __________ stimulates the production of gastric juice in the stomach

    (a) Gastrin   (b) Enterokinase   (c) Rennin   (d) Digestin

Directions: Q. No. 13-16 contain five sub-parts each. You are expected to answer **any four** sub-parts in these questions.

13. Read the following and answer any four questions from 13 (i) to 13 (v).

A lens is a piece of transparent material with two refracting surfaces such that at least one is curved and refractive index of used material is different from that of the surroundings.

Convex Lens : A thin spherical lens with refractive index greater than that of surrounding behaves as a convergent or convex lens i.e. converges parallel rays. Its central (i.e. paraxial) portion is thicker than marginal one.

Concave Lens : If the central portion of a lens (with $\mu_L > \mu_M$) is thinner than marginal, it diverges parallel rays and behaves as a divergent or a concave lens.

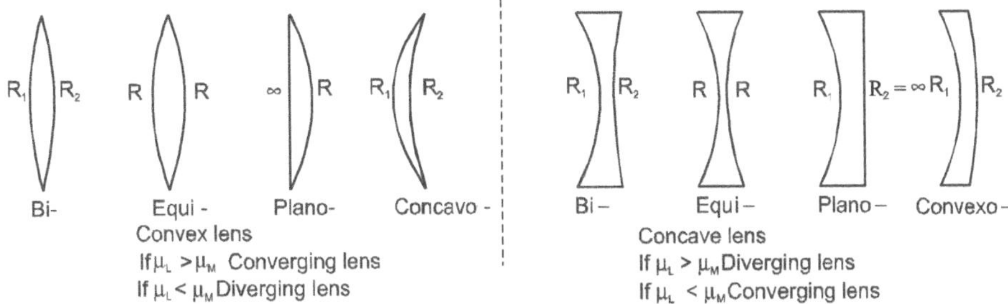

(i) A thin spherical lens with refractive index greater than that of surrounding behaves as a

    (a) Convex lens   (b) Concave lens

    (c) Convexo-concave   (d) None of the above

(ii) When sun rays are focussed on a convex lens, a sharp, bright spot is observed at its focus. What does this spot indicate?

    (a) The real image of the sun

    (b) The virtual image of the sun

    (c) An optical illusion produced by the convex lens

    (d) The magnified image of the sun

(iii) The focal length of concave and convex lens are respectively

    (a) +(vc) & I (ve)   (b) –(ve) & –(ve)

    (c) –(ve) & +(ve)   (d) +(ve) & –(ve)

(iv) Which of the following ray diagram is correct?

(a)
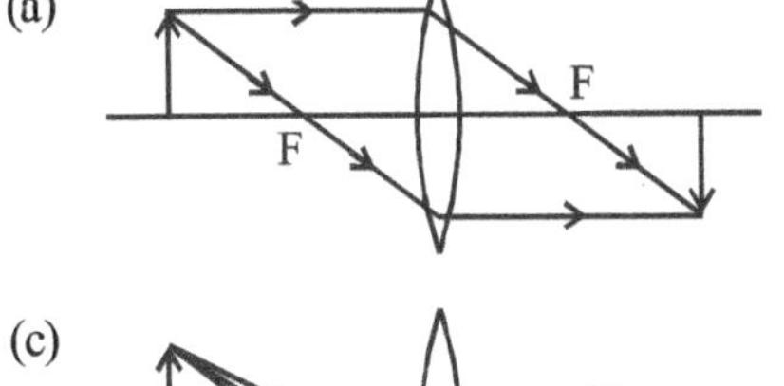

(b)
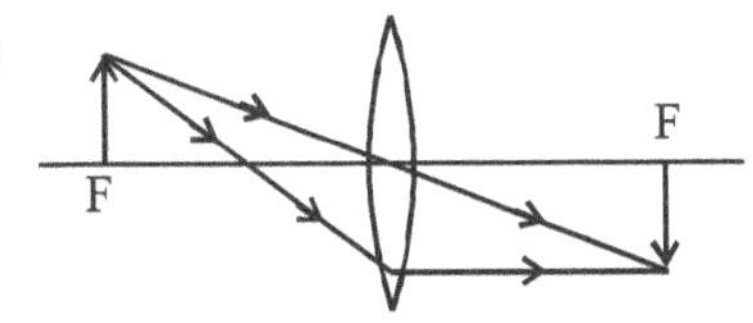

(c)
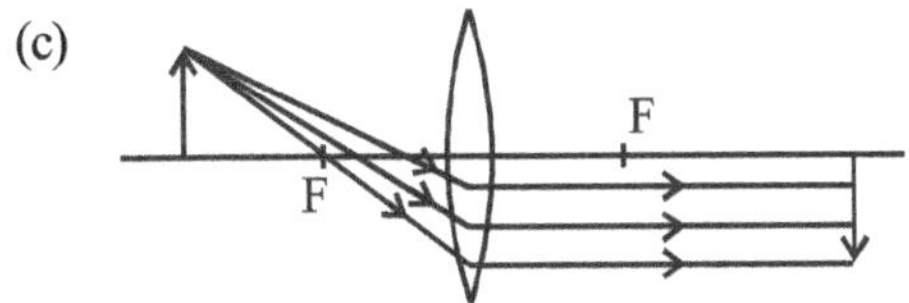

(d)
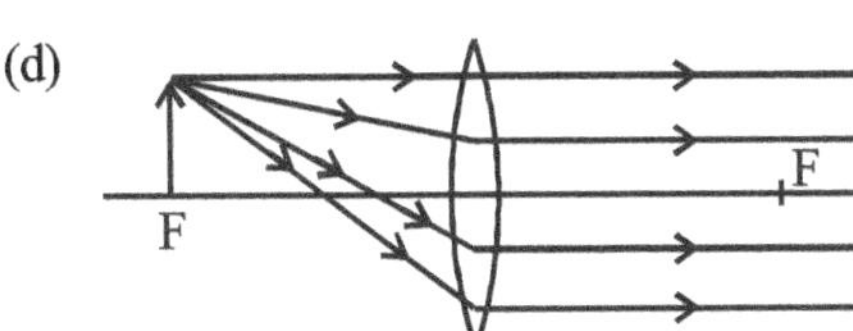

(v) Which of the following ray diagrams is correct for the ray of light incident on a lens shown in figure?

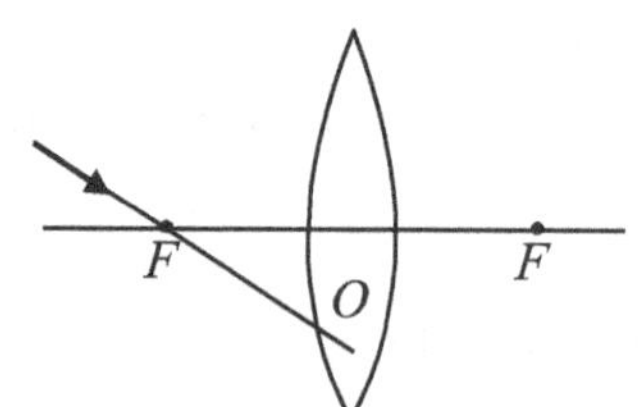

(a) 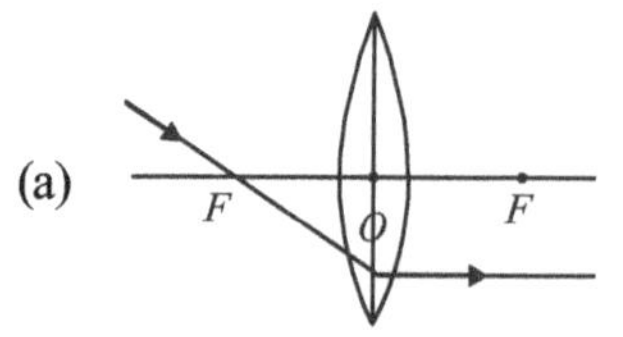   (b) 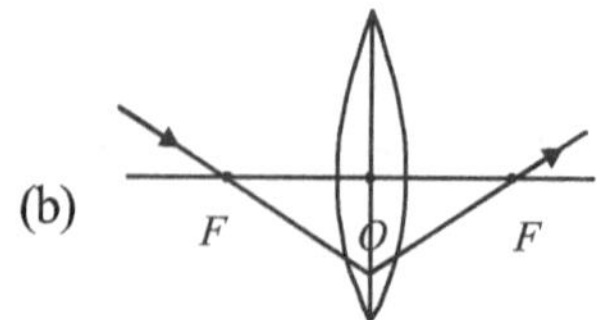

(c) 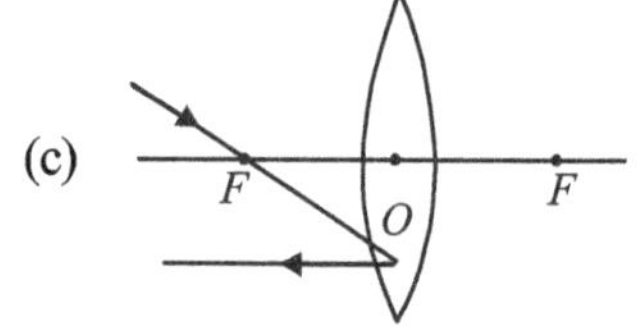   (d) 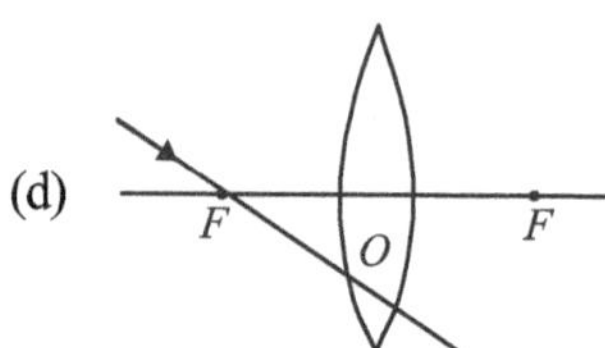

14. **Read the following and attempt any four questions from 14(i) to 14(v).**

Acids produce hydrogen ions, $H^+(aq)$, in solution, which are responsible for their acidic properties. Hydrogen ions cannot exist alone, but they exist after combining with water molecules. when a base is dissolved in water. Bases generate hydroxide (OH^-) ions in water. Bases which are soluble in water are called alkalis. that all acids generate $H^+(aq)$ and all bases generate $OH^-(aq)$,

Acid + Base $\longrightarrow$ Salt + Water

(i) Ammonium hydroxide is a weak base because

  (a) it has low vapour pressure   (b) it is only slightly ionised

  (c) it is not a hydroxide of any metal   (d) it has low density

(ii) The poisonous effect of acid present in stings of bees and ants can be neutralised by use of a solution that contains

  (a) acetic acid   (b) formic acid

  (c) sodium hydroxide   (d) sodium chloride.

(iii) Which of the following is an alkali ?

  (a) $Ca(OH)_2$ (b) KOH   (c) $Mg(OH)_2$ (d) $CaCO_3$

(iv) Acids and bases are important because of

  (a) their use in industry   (b) their effects on human health

  (c) their effect on farmer's crop   (d) All the above are correct.

(v) Which of following compound is alkaline in aqueous medium.

  (a) Na_2CO_3 (b) NaCl   (c) H_2CO_3 (d) $CuSO_4$

15. **Read the following and answer any four questions from 15(i) to 15(v).**

Elements can be classified as metals or non-metals on the basis of their properties. The easiest way to start grouping substances is by comparing their physical properties. Metals, in their pure state, have a shining surface. This property is called metallic luster. metals are generally hard. The hardness varies from metal to metal. some metals that are used for making cooking vessels.

(i) Metals generally are

    (a) reducing agents   (b) oxidising agent

    (c) both oxidising and reducing agents   (d) None of these

(ii) The most abundant metal in the earth's crust is -

    (a) iron   (b) copper   (c) aluminium   (d) mercury

(iii) The metal that reacts with cold water is -

    (a) mercury   (b) sodium   (c) zinc   (d) tungsten

(iv) Metal present in chloroplast is

    (a) Iron   (b) Copper   (c) Magnesium   (d) Cobalt

(v) Which of the following metal(s) catch fire on reaction with water?

    (a) Sodium   (b) Potassium   (c) Magnesium   (d) both (a) and (b)

16. **Read the following and answer any four questions from 16 (i) to 16 (v).**

These contraceptive methods fall in a number of categories. One category is the creation of a mechanical barrier so that sperm does not reach the egg. Condoms on the penis or similar coverings worn in the vagina can serve this purpose. Another category of contraceptives acts by changing the hormonal balance of the body so that eggs are not released and fertilisation cannot occur. These drugs commonly need to be taken orally as pills. However, since they change hormonal balances, they can cause side-effects too. Other contraceptive devices such as the loop or the copper-T are placed in the uterus to prevent pregnancy. Again, they can cause side effects due to irritation of the uterus. If the vas deferens in the male is blocked, sperm transfer will be prevented. If the fallopian tube in the female is blocked, the egg will not be able to reach the uterus. In both cases fertilisation will not take place. Surgical methods can be used to create such blocks. While surgical methods are safe in the long run, surgery itself can cause infections and other problems if not performed properly. Surgery can also be used for removal of unwanted pregnancies. These may be misused by people who do not want a particular child, as happens in illegal sex-selective abortion of female foetuses. For a healthy society, the female-male sex ratio must be maintained. Because of reckless female foeticides, child sex ratio is declining at an alarming rate in some sections of our society, although prenatal sex determination has been prohibited by law.

(i) What is the function of copper-T?

    (a) stop oblituation of the blastocoel   (b) checks mutation

    (c) stops fertilization   (d) Stops zygote formation

(ii) Test tube baby means a baby born when

    (a) developed in a test tube

    (b) ovum is fertilized externally and there after implanted in the uterus

    (c) it is developed through the tissue culture method

    (d) developed from a non-fertilized egg.

(iii) Through amniocentesis, foetal cells can be tested for detecting varous diseases if foetus by

    (a) DNA Analysis   (b) Karotype

    (c) Enzyme production   (d) All of these

(iv) Which one of the following is tested by the technique of amniocentesis?

    (a) chromosomal abnormalities in a foetus   (b) biochemical abnormalities in a foetus

    (c) errors of metabolism in a foetus   (d) all the above

(v) Which of the following is a method of birth control?

    (a) GIFT   (b) IUDs   (c) IVE-ET   (d) HTF

Directions: Q. No. 17-20 contain five sub-parts each. You are expected to answer **any four** sub-parts in these questions.

---

17. **Read the following and answer any four questions from 17 (i) to 17 (v).**

For a conductor of length L carrying a current of I in a field B the force experienced by the conductor

$$\vec{F} = I\,\vec{L} \times \vec{B}$$

If the current-carrying conductor in the form of a loop of any arbitrary shape is placed in a uniform field, then, $\vec{F} = 0$ i.e., the net magnetic force on a current loop in a uniform magnetic field is always zero. Here it must be kept in mind that in this situation different parts of the loop may experience elemental force due to which the loop may be under tension or may experience a torque.

Direction of force can be determined by fleming's left hand rule, right hand palm rule or screw rule.

(i) The direction of induced current is obtained by

    (a) Fleming's left hand rule

    (b) Maxwell's cork-screw rule

    (c) Ampere's rule

    (d) Fleming's right hand rule

(ii) An electron moving with uniform velocity in x-direction enters a region of uniform magnetic field along y-direction. Which of the following physical quantity(ies) is (are) non-zero and remain constant?

    I.   Velocity of the electron

    II.   Magnitude of the momentum of the electron.

    III. Force on the electron.

    IV. The kinetic energy of electron.

    (a) Only I and II.   (b) Only III and IV.   (c) All four   (d) Only II and IV.

(iii) Which of the following can produce a magnetic field?

    (a) Electric charges at rest

    (b) Electric charges in motion

    (c) Only by permanent magnets

    (d) Electric charges whether at rest or in motion

(iv) A wire is lying horizontally in the north-south direction and there is a horizontal magnetic field pointing towards the east. Some positive charges in the wire move north and an equal number of negative charges move south. The direction of force on the wire will be

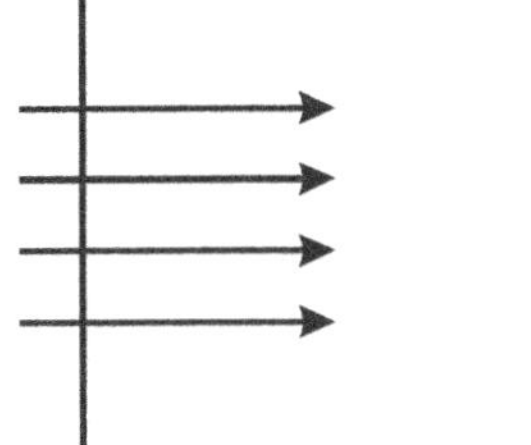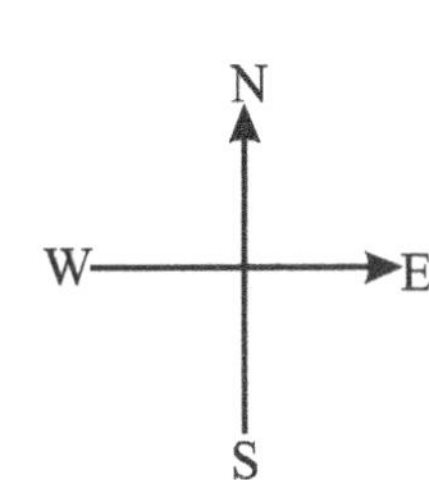

(a) east

(b) down, into the page

(c) up, out of the page

(d) west

(v) Four situations are given below-

I.   An infinitely long wire carrying current

II. A rectangular loop carrying current

III. A solenoid of finite length carrying current

IV. A circular loop carrying current.

In which of the above cases will the magnetic field produced be like that of a bar magnet?

(a) I   (b) I and III   (c) Only III   (d) Only IV

18. **Read the following and attempt any four questions from 18(i) to 18(v).**

Almost all metals combine with oxygen to form metal oxides. when copper is heated in air, it combines with oxygen to form copper(II) oxide, a black oxide. aluminium forms aluminium oxide. copper oxide reacts with hydrochloric acid. metal oxides are basic in nature. But some metal oxides, such as aluminium oxide, zinc oxide, etc., show both acidic as well as basic behaviour. Such metal oxides which react with both acids as well as bases to produce salts and water are known as amphoteric oxides.

(i) Which of them is solid at room temperature but becomes liquid in the palm?

(a) Hg   (b) Na   (c) Mg   (d) Ga

(ii) When sodium is exposed in air, what products will be formed

(a) Na_2O (b) NaOH   (c) Na_2CO_3 (d) All of these

(iii) When a metal is added to dilute HCl solution, there is no evolution of gas. Metal is

(a) K   (b) Na   (c) Ag   (d) Zn

(iv) $Zn + H_2O \, (Steam) \longrightarrow A + B,$

In the equation A and B are -

(a) Zn, H only   (b) ZnH_2 and O_2

(c) ZnO_2 & O_2 (d) ZnO & H_2

(v) Copper sulphate solution can be safely kept in a container made of

(a) aluminium   (b) lead

(c) silver   (d) zinc

19. **Read the following and answer any four questions from 19(i) to 19(v).**
    The Modern Periodic Table has 18 vertical columns known as 'groups' and 7 horizontal rows known as 'periods. the number of valence shell electrons increases by one unit, as the atomic number increases by one unit on moving from left to right in a period. Each period marks a new electronic shell getting filled. The position of an element in the Periodic Table tells us about its chemical reactivity. The term atomic size refers to the radius of an atom.. the atomic size increases down the group while it decreases on moving left to right in the periodic table.

    (i) Amongst the following elements which has the largest atomic size?

    (a) magnesium   (b) phosphorus

    (c) silicon   (d) chlorine

    (ii) Which is incorred order of size?

    (a) $Na > Na^+$ (b) $Na^+ > Mg^{2+}$

    (c) $Cl^- > Cl$ (d) $F^- > O^{2-}$

    (iii) Which of the following is the correct order of sizes?

    (a) $I^- > I^+ > I$ (b) $I^- > I^+ > I$

    (c) $I > I^+ > I^-$ (d) $I^+ > I^- > I$

    (iv) The element with electronic configuration 2, 8, 6 is

    (a) metallic with valency 2   (b) non-metallic with valency 2

    (c) metalloid with valency 2   (d) none of these

    (v) Increasing order of atomic radii is

    (a) $Ca < Na < Mg$ (b) $Mg < Ca < Na$

    (c) $Mg < Na < Ca$ (d) $Na < Mg < Ca$

20. **Read the following and answer any four questions from 20 (i) to 20 (v).**
    Asexual Reproduction:
    Organisms such as Hydra use regenerative cells for reproduction in the process of budding. In Hydra, a bud develops as an outgrowth due to repeated cell division at one specific site. These buds develop into tiny individuals and when fully mature, detach from the parent body and become new independent individuals. Many fully differentiated organisms have the ability to give rise to new individual organisms from their body parts. That is, if the individual is somehow cut or broken up into many pieces, many of these pieces grow into separate individuals. For example, simple animals like *Hydra* and *Planaria* can be cut into any number of pieces and each piece grows into a complete organism. This is known as regeneration. Regeneration is carried out by specialised cells. These cells proliferate and make large numbers of cells. From this mass of cells, different cells undergo changes to become various cell types and tissues. These changes take place in an organised sequence referred to as development. However, regeneration is not the same as reproduction, since most organisms would not normally depend on being cut up to be able to reproduce. The property of vegetative propagation is used in methods such as layering or grafting to grow many plants like sugarcane, roses, or grapes for agricultural purposes. Plants raised by vegetative propagation can bear flowers and fruits earlier than those produced from seeds. Such methods also make possible the propagation of plants such as banana, orange, rose and jasmine that have lost the capacity

to produce seeds. Another advantage of vegetative propagation is that all plants produced are genetically similar enough to the parent plant to have all its characteristics. For unicellular organisms, cell division, or fission, leads to the creation of new individuals. Many different patterns of fission have been observed. Many bacteria and protozoa simply split into two equal halves during cell division. In organisms, such as *Amoeba*, the splitting of the two cells during division can take place in any plane.

(i) During favourable conditions, Amoeba reproduces by

    (a) multiple fission   (b) binary fission

    (c) budding   (d) fragmentation

(ii) A feature of reproduction that is common to Amoeba, Yeast and *Spirogyra* is that

    (a) they reproduce asexually   (b) they are all unicellular

    (c) they reproduce only sexually   (d) they are all multicellular

(iii) The ability of a cell to divide into several cells during reproduction in *Plasmodium* is celled

    (a) budding   (b) multiple fission

    (c) binary fission   (d) reduction division

(iv) Bryophyllum can be propagated vegetatively by the

    (a) stem   (b) leaf

    (c) root   (d) flower

(v) In a potato, vegetative propagation takes place by:

    (a) root   (b) leaf

    (c) stem tuber   (d) grafting

Directions: Q. No. 21-24 contain five sub-parts each. You are expected to answer **any four** sub-parts in these questions.

---

21. **Read the following and answer any four questions from 21 (i) to 21 (v).**

The heart is a muscular organ which is as big as our fist. Because both oxygen and carbon dioxide have to be transported by the blood, the heart has different chambers to prevent the oxygen-rich blood from mixing with the blood containing carbon dioxide. The carbon dioxide-rich blood has to reach the lungs for the carbon dioxide to be removed, and the oxygenated blood from the lungs has to be brought back to the heart. This oxygen-rich blood is then pumped to the rest of the body. We can follow this process step by step. Oxygen-rich blood from the lungs comes to the thin-walled upper chamber of the heart on the left, the left atrium. The left atrium relaxes when it is collecting this blood. It then contracts, while the next chamber, the left ventricle, expands, so that the blood is transferred to it. When the muscular left ventricle contracts in its turn, the blood is pumped out to the body. De-oxygenated blood comes from the body to the upper chamber on the right, the right atrium, as it expands. As the right atrium contracts, the corresponding lower chamber, the right ventricle, dilates. This transfers blood to the right ventricle, which in turn pumps it to the lungs for oxygenation. Since ventricles have to pump blood into various organs, they have thicker muscular walls than the atria do. Valves ensure that blood does not flow backwards when the atria or ventricles contract.

(i) Which of the following has the thickest wall?

(a) Right ventricle   (b) Left ventricle

(c) Right atrium   (d) Left atrium

(ii) _________ carries deoxygenated blood to the lungs from the right ventricle.

(a) Pulmonary artery   (b) Pulmonary vein

(c) Aorta   (d) None of the above

(iii) Humans use haemoglobin to carry oxygen in their blood. Similarly, mollusks and crustaceans use _________ to carry oxygen iin their blood.

(a) Hemovanadin   (b) Hemerthrin

(c) Haemoglobin   (d) Hemocyanin

(iv) _________ forms clots when blood vessels get damaged.

(a) Hemovanadin   (b) Hemerthrin

(c) Haemoglobin   (d) Hemocyanin

(v) The nearest organ to which the heart supplies oxygenated blood is

(a) Lung   (b) Stomach

(c) Intestine   (d) Heart itself

22. **Read the following and attempt any four questions from 22 (i) to 22 (v).**

The phenomenon of decomposition of the white light into its seven component colours when passing through a prism or through a transparent object delimited by non parallel surfaces is called dispersion of light. A beam of light containing all the visible spectrum of the light is white, because the sum of all the colors generates the white color. The light is decomposed in all the component colours, Violet, Indigo, Blue, Green, Yellow, Orange and Red, called as VIBGYOR. The band of the coloured components of a light beam is called its spectrum. The phenomenon can be explained by thinking that light of different colours (different wavelengths) has different velocities while travelling in a medium $v_m = f\lambda_m$.

Hence, the change in velocity of light observed when the light passes from the air to the glass, depends on the wavelength.

(i) A prism ABC (with BC as base) is placed in different orientations. A narrow beam of white light is incident on the prism as shown in figure. In which of the following cases, after dispersion, the third colour from the top corresponds to the colour of the sky?

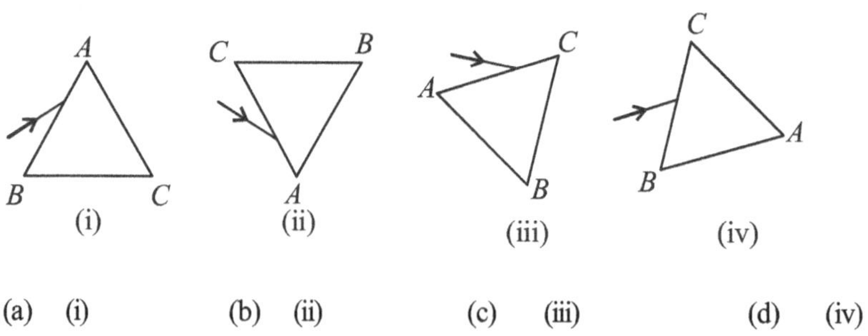

(a) (i)   (b) (ii)   (c) (iii)   (d) (iv)

(ii) Which of the following statements is correct regarding the propagation of light of different colours of white light in air?

(a) Red light moves fastest

(b) Blue light moves faster than green light

(c) All the colours of the white light move with the same speed

(d) Yellow light moves with the mean speed as that of the red and the violet light

(iii) When white light is allowed to pass through a glass prism, which colour deviates the least?

(a) Violet   (b) Red   (c) Green   (d) Orange

(iv) When white light is allowed to pass through a glass prism, which colour deviates the most?

(a) Indigo   (b) Green   (c) Red   (d) Violet

(v) For a prism material, refractive index is highest for

(a) Red   (b) Yellow   (c) Orange   (d) Violet

23. Read the following and answer any four questions from 23(i) to 23(v).

Chemical reactions involve the breaking and making of bonds between atoms to produce new substances. during a chemical reaction atoms of one element do not change into those of another element. Nor do atoms disappear from the mixture or appear from elsewhere. There are certain types of reactions. Reactions in which a single product is formed from two or more reactants is known as a combination reaction. Decomposition reactions are the reactions in which a compound breaks down into simpler compounds. Displacement and double displacement reactions are the one in which an atom or group of atom is replaced by another. Another type of reaction is redox reactions in which simultaneous oxidation and reduction takes place.

(i) Which of the following reactions involved the combination of two element ?

(a) $CaO + CO_2 \longrightarrow CaCO_3$

(b) $4Na + O_2 \longrightarrow 2Na_2O$

(c) $SO_2 + \frac{1}{2}O_2 \longrightarrow SO_3$

(d) $NH_3 + HCl \longrightarrow NH_4Cl$

(ii) Consider the reaction

$Fe_2O_3 + 2Al \longrightarrow Al_2O_3 + 2Fe$

The above reaction is an example of

(a) combination reaction

(b) double displacement reaction

(c) decomposition reaction

(d) simple displacement reaction

(iii) The equation

$Mg\,(s) + CuO\,(s) \longrightarrow MgO\,(s) + Cu\,(s)$ represents

(i) decomposition reaction

(ii) displacement reaction

(iii) combination reaction

(iv) double displacement reaction

(v) redox reaction

(a) (i) and (ii)

(b) (iii) and (iv)

(c) (ii) and (v)

(d) (iv) and (v)

(iv) Which of the following is a decomposition reaction?

 (a) $2HgO \xrightarrow{\text{heat}} 2Hg + O_2$

 (b) $CaCO_3 \xrightarrow{\text{heat}} CaO + CO_2$

 (c) $2H_2O \xrightarrow{\text{electrolysis}} H_2 + O_2$

 (d) All of these

(v) $CuO + H_2 \longrightarrow H_2O + Cu$ reaction is an example of -

 (a) redox reaction   (b) synthesis reaction

 (c) neutralisation   (d) analysis reaction

24. **Read the following and answer any four questions from 24 (i) to 24 (v).**

The female germ-cells or eggs are made in the ovaries. They are also responsible for the production of some hormones. When a girl is born, the ovaries already contain thousands of immature eggs. On reaching puberty, some of these start maturing. One egg is produced every month by one of the ovaries. The egg is carried from the ovary to the womb through a thin oviduct or fallopian tube. The two oviducts unite into an elastic bag-like structure known as the uterus. The uterus opens into the vagina through the cervix. The sperms enter through the vaginal passage during sexual intercourse. They travel upwards and reach the oviduct where they may encounter the egg. The fertilised egg, the zygote, gets implanted in the lining of the uterus, and starts dividing. The mother's body is designed to undertake the development of the child. Hence the uterus prepares itself every month to receive and nurture the growing embryo. The lining thickens and is richly supplied with blood to nourish the growing embryo. The embryo gets nutrition from the mother's blood with the help of a special tissue called placenta. This is a disc which is embedded in the uterine wall. It contains villi on the embryo's side of the tissue. On the mother's side are blood spaces, which surround the villi. This provides a large surface area for glucose and oxygen to pass from the mother to the embryo. The developing embryo will also generate waste substances which can be removed by transferring them into the mother's blood through the placenta. The development of the child inside the mother's body takes approximately nine months. The child is born as a result of rhythmic contractions of the muscles in the uterus.

(i) Which one of the following causes the mammary glands to enlarge at puberty?

 (a) Testosterone   (b) Progesterone

 (c) Estrogen   (d) Oxytocin

(ii) What is the inner lining of the uterus called?

 (a) Cervix   (b) Oviduct

 (c) Endometrium   (d) Fimbriate

(iii) Which of the following comes under the functions of female reproductive system?

 (a) formation of ova   (b) lactation

 (c) parturition   (d) all of the above

(iv) The figure given below depicts a diagrammatic sectional view of the female reproductive system of humans. Which one set of three parts out of A-F have been correctly identified?

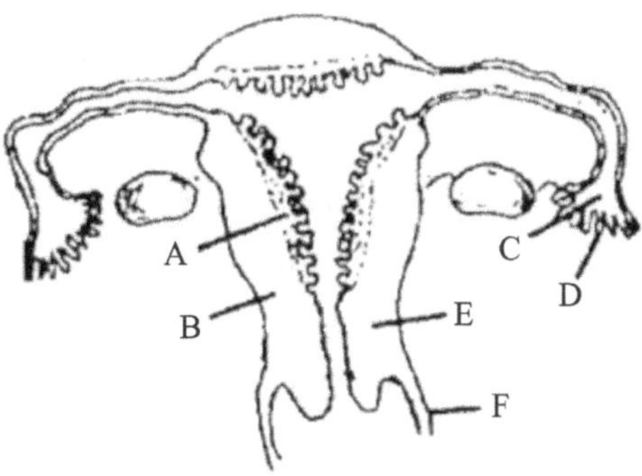

(a) C-Infundibulum, D-Fimbriae, E-Cervix

(b) D Oviducal funnol, E Utcrus, F Ccrvix

(c) A-Perimetrium, B-Myometxium, C-Fallopian tube

(d) B Endomctrium, C Infundibulum, D Fimbriac

(v) The part of fallopian tube closest to the ovary is

    (a) isthmus   (b) infundibulum

    (c) cervix   (d) ampulla

Directions: Q. No. 25-28 contain five sub-parts each. You are expected to answer **any four** sub-parts in these questions.

---

25. **Read the following and answer any four questions from 25 (i) to 25 (v).**

The rate at which electric energy is dissipated or consumed in an electric circuit. This is termed as electric power,

$$P = IV, \text{According to Ohm's law } V = IR$$

We can express the power dissipated in the alternative forms $P = I^2 R = \dfrac{V^2}{R}$

If 100W – 220V is written on the bulb then it means that the bulb will consume 100 joule in one second if used at the potential difference of 220 volts. The value of electricity consumed in houses is decided on the basis of the total electric energy used. Electric power tells us about the electric energy used per second not the total electric energy.

The total energy used in a circuit = power of the electric circuit × time.

(i) Which of the following terms does not represent electrical power in a circuit?

    (a) I^2R (b) IR^2 (c) VI   (d) V^2/R

(ii) An electric bulb is rated 220V and 100W. When it is operated on 110V, the power consumed will be–

    (a) 100 W   (b) 75 W   (c) 50 W   (d) 25 W

(iii) Two conducting wires of the same material and of equal lengths and equal diameters are first connected in sereis and then in parallel in an electric circuit. The ratio of heat produced in series and in parallel combinations would be–

    (a) 1 : 2   (b) 2 : 1   (c) 1 : 4   (d) 4 : 1

(iv) In an electrical circuit three incandescent bulbs. A, B and C of rating 40 W, 60 W and 100 W, respectively are connected in parallel to an electric source. Which of the following is likely to happen regarding their brightness?

(a)   Brightness of all the bulbs will be the same

(b)   Brightness of bulb A will be the maximum

(c)   Brightness of bulb B will be more than that of A

(d)   Brightness of bulb C will be less than that of B

(v) In an electrical circuit, two resistors of 2Ω and 4Ω respectively are connected in series to a 6V battery. The heat dissipated by the 4Ω resistor in 5s will be

(a)   5 J   (b)   10 J   (c)   20 J   (d)   30 J

26. **Read the following and attempt any four questions from 26 (i) to 26 (v).**

When sunlight enters the earth atmosphere, air and water vapour molecules will absorb part of the light and reradiate it to all directions. This is called scattering.

According to Rayleigh's law of scattering the amount of scattered light $\propto \dfrac{1}{(\text{wavelength})^4}$ so that the wavelength of violet, blue and indigo is small as compared to the rest of the colours. So sky appears blue in colour.

(i) At noon the sun appears white as

(a)   light is least scattered   (b)   all the colours of the white light are scattered away

(c)   blue colour is scattered the most   (d)   red colour is scattered the most

(ii) The wavelengths of two light sources A and B are X and Y. The ratio of light scattered from A and B is

(a) $\dfrac{X}{Y}$ (b) $\dfrac{X^4}{Y^4}$ (c) $\dfrac{X^3}{Y^3}$ (d) $\dfrac{X^2}{Y^2}$

(iii) The clear sky appears blue, because

(a)   blue light gets absorbed in the atmosphere

(b)   ultraviolet radiations are absorbed in the atmosphere

(c)   blue lights get scattered more

(d)   light of all other colours is scattered more than the violet and blue colour lights by the atmosphere

(iv) The danger signals installed at the top of tall buildings are red in colour. These can be easily seen from a distance because among all other colours, the red light

(a)   is scattered the most by smoke or fog

(b)   is scattered the least by smoke or fog

(c)   is absorbed the most by smoke or fog

(d)   moves fastest in air

(v) The bluish colour of water in deep sea is due to

(a)   the presence of algae and other plants found in water   (b)   reflection of sky in water

(c)   scattering of light   (d)   absorption of light by the sea

27. **Read the following and answer any four questions from 27 (i) to (v).**
Within the lungs, the passage divides into smaller and smaller tubes which finally terminate in balloon-like structures which are called alveoli. The alveoli provide a surface where the exchange of gases can take place. The walls of the alveoli contain an extensive network of blood-vessels. As we have seen in earlier years, when we breathe in, we lift our ribs and flatten our diaphragm, and the chest cavity becomes larger as a result. Because of this, air is sucked into the lungs and fills the expanded alveoli. The blood brings carbon dioxide from the rest of the body for release into the alveoli, and the oxygen in the alveolar air is taken up by blood in the alveolar blood vessels to be transported to all the cells in the body. During the breathing cycle, when air is taken in and let out, the lungs always contain a residual volume of air so that there is sufficient time for oxygen to be absorbed and for the carbon dioxide to be released.

(i)   In which part of the respiratory system, gaseous exchange takes place?

   (a) Alveoli   (b) Pharynx   (c) Larynx   (d) Trachea

(ii) .... is located between two pleural sacs and is the central compartment of the thoracic cavity?

   (a) Hilum   (b) Pleura   (c) Mediastinum   (d) Thoracic cage

(iii) Which of the following are parts of the human respiratory system?

   (a) Trachea   (b) Diaphragm   (c) The lungs   (d) All of the above

(iv) The tiny air sacs present in human lungs is called ....

   (a) Alveoli   (b) Bronchus   (c) Bronchioles   (d) All of the above

(v)   The exchange of gases between the external environmental and the lungs ....

   (a) Respiration   (b) External respiration

   (c) Cellular respiration   (d) None of the above

28. **Read the following and answer any four questions from 28 (i) to 28 (v).**

Food, clothes, medicines, books, or many of the things are all based on this versatile element carbon. In addition, all living structures are carbon based. The earth's crust has only 0.02% carbon in the form of minerals. The element carbon occurs in different forms in nature with widely varying physical properties. Both diamond and graphite are formed by carbon atoms, the difference lies in the manner in which the carbon atoms are bonded to one another. Carbon has the unique ability to form bonds with other atoms of carbon, giving rise to large molecules. This property is called catenation.

(i)   From the given alternatives, whose chemical and physical properties are *not* same?

   (a) Graphite and Diamond   (b) Phosphorous and Sulphur

   (c) Carbon and Hydrogen   (d) Methyl alcohol and Acetic acid

(ii) Which of the following statements is not correct?

   (a) Graphite is much less dense than diamond

   (b) Graphite is black and soft

   (c) Graphite has low melting point   (d) Graphite feels smooth and slippery

(iii) Which of the following are isomers?

   (a) Butane and isobutene   (b) Ethane and ethene

   (c) Propane and propyne   (d) Butane and isobutane

(iv) Which one of the following is not an allotrope of carbon?

    (a)   Soot   (b) Graphite   (c) Diamond   (d) Carborundum

(v) Pentane has the molecular formula C_5H_{12}. It has

    (a)   5 covalent bonds   (b) 12 covalent bonds

    (c) 16 covalent bonds   (d) 17 covalent bonds

Directions: Q. No. 29-32 contain five sub-parts each. You are expected to answer **any four** sub-parts in these questions.

---

29. **Read the following and answer any four questions from 29 (i) to 29 (v).**

Mendel used a number of contrasting visible characters of garden peas - round/wrinkled seeds, tall/short plants, white/violet flowers and so on. He took pea plants with different characteristics - a tall plant and a short plant, produced progeny from them, and calculated the percentages of tall or short progeny. In the first place, there were no halfway characteristics in this first generation, or F1 progeny - no 'medium-height' plants. All plants were tall. This meant that only one of the parental traits was seen, not some mixture of the two. Mendelian experiments test this by getting both the parental plants and these F1 tall plants to reproduce by self-pollination. The progeny of the parental plants are, of course, all tall. However, the second-generation, or F2, progeny of the F1 tall plants are not all tall. Instead, one quarter of them are short. This indicates that both the tallness and shortness traits were inherited in the F1 plants, but only the tallness trait was expressed. Thus, two copies of the trait are inherited in each sexually reproducing organism. These two may be identical, or may be different, depending on the parentage.

(i) What is the maximum number of allele that monohydrid cross consider?

    (a) 1   (b) 2

    (c) 8   (d) 8

(ii) The monohybrid phenotypic and genotypic ratio is same in the case of _________ .

    (a) Multiple allele   (b) Codominance

    (c) Incomplete dominance   (d) Normal dominance recessive relation

(iii) If a true breeding tall pea plant is crossed with a true breeding short pea plant, what will be the phenotype of the F1 generation?

    (a) All short   (b) All tall

    (c) 3:1 short: tall   (d) 1:3 short: tall

(iv) Who is the father of genetics?

    (a) Peabody   (b) Starsky

    (c) Hutch   (d) Mendel

(v) If a pea plant were homozygous recessive for height how would its alleles be represented?

    (a) TT   (b) Tt

    (c) tt   (d) tT

30. **Read the following and attempt any four questions from 30 (i) to 30 (v).**

There are 18 groups in periodic table & each group is a independent group. All the elements present in a group have same electronic configuration of the atoms. The physical and chemical properties of elements depend on the number of valence electrons. Elements present in the same group have the same number of valence electrons. Atomic radius & ionic radius are the periodic properties which are directly or indirectly related to the electronic configuration of their atoms & shows gradation on moving down a group or along a period. Ionization enthalpy is the minimum amount of energy which is needed to remove the most loosly boundelectron from a neutral isolated gaseous atom to form a cation. On moving down a group the ionization enthalpies generally decreses due to increase in atomic size & screening effect which is more than to compensate the effect of increase in nuclear charge.Consequently the electron becomes less & less tightly held by the nucleus as we move down the group.

(i) All the members in a group in long form of periodic table have the same

  (a) valence   (b) number of valence electrons

  (c) chemical properties   (d) All of these

(ii) The element with smallest size in group 13 is

  (a) beryllium   (b) carbon

  (c) aluminium   (d) boron

(iii) The Anion O^{2-} is isoelectronic with

  (a) F^{+} (b) F^{-}

  (c) N^{2-} (d) N^{+3}

(iv) Which of these choices is not a family of elements?

  (a) Halogens   (b) Metals

  (c) Inert gases   (d) All of these

(v) The element which has least tendency to lose electron is

  (a) H   (b) Li

  (c) He   (d) Ne

31. **Read the following and answer any four questions from 31 (i) to 31 (v).**

In everyday life we deal with many compounds that chemists classify as acids. For example, orange juice and grapcfruit juice contain citric acid. In any chemistry laboratory, we find acids such as hydrochloric acid, sulfuric acid, and nitric acid. These acids are called mineral acids because they can be prepared from naturally occurring compounds called minerals. Mineral acids are generally stronger than household acids. Acids taste sour. Citric acid is responsible for the sour taste of lemons, limes, grapefruits, and oranges. Acetic acid is responsible for the sour taste of vinegar. Acids turn litmus (or indicator papers) red.

(i) Some fruits like mango, lemon, raw grapes, orange, etc., have a sour taste due to the presence of:

  (a) Acetic acid   (b) Citric acid

  (c) Lactic acid   (d) Oxatic acid

(ii) Which of the following indicators turn red in an acidic solution?

(A) Phenolphthalein

(B) Litmus

(C) Turmeric

(D) Methyl orange

Choose the correct option:

(a) (A) and (B)

(b) (B) and (C)

(c) only (B)

(d) (B) and (D)

(iii) Dilute acid does not produce carbon dioxide on being treated with:

(a) Marble

(b) Lime

(c) Baking soda

(d) Limestone

(iv) Which of the following salt will give acidic solution when dissolved in water?

(a) NH_4Cl

(b) $NaCl$

(c) Na_2CO_3

(d) CH_3COONa

(v) An ant's sting can be treated with ....which will neutralise the effect of the chemical injected by the ant's sting into our skin.

Choose the correct option from the following to be filled in the blank space:

(a) Methanoic acid

(b) Formic acid

(c) Baking soda

(d) Caustic soda

32. Read the following and answer any four questions from 32 (i) to 32 (v).

If focal length of a lens is measured in metre (m) then its reciprocal gives the power (P) of the lens.

i.e., Power of a lens, $\quad P = \dfrac{1}{f \text{ (in m)}}$

The S.I. unit of power is diopter (D).

Power of a combination of lenses: If a number of lenses are placed in close contact with each other, then the power of the combination of lenses is equal to the algebraic sum of the powers of individual lenses.

i.e. $P = P_1 + P_2 + ...P_n$.

(i) What is the power of a concave lens whose focal length is -75.0 cm?

(a) $1.33\,D$

(b) $-13.3\,D$

(c) $13.3\,D$

(d) $-1.33\,D$

(ii) A convex lens has a focal length of 0.5 m. It has to be combined with a second lens, so that the combination has a power of 1.5 diopter. Which of the following could be the second lens?

(a) A concave lens of focal length 2 m.

(b) Another convex lens of focal length 0.5 m.

(c) A concave lens of focal length 0.5 m.

(d) A convex lens of focal length 2 m.

(iii) Which of the following statements is true?

(a) A convex lens has 4 dioptre power having a focal length 0.25 m

(b) A convex lens has 4 dioptre power having a focal length -0.25 m

(c) A concave lens has 4 dioptre power having a focal length 0.25 m

(d) A concave lens has 4 dioptre power having a focal length -0.25 m

(iv) Find the focal length of a lens of power –2D. What type of lens is this?

    (a)   –50 cm concave   (b)   +50 cm, convex

    (c)   +100 cm, concave   (d)   –100 cm, convex

(v) Find the power of a concave lens of focal length 2 m?

    (a)   –0.5 D   (b)   +0.5 D

    (c)   1 D   (d)   –1 D

Directions: Q. No. 33-36 contain five sub-parts each. You are expected to answer **any four** sub-parts in these questions.

---

33. Read the following and answer any four questions from 33 (i) to 33 (v).

If the egg is not fertilised, it lives for about one day. Since the ovary releases one egg every month, the uterus also prepares itself every month to receive a fertilised egg. Thus its lining becomes thick and spongy. This would be required for nourishing the embryo if fertilisation had taken place. Now, however, this lining is not needed any longer. So, the lining slowly breaks and comes out through the vagina as blood and mucous. This cycle takes place roughly every month and is known as menstruation. It usually lasts for about two to eight days.

(i) In the process of fertilization, this is true

    (a)   the entry of sperm activiates the egg for completing meiosis

    (b)   only one sperm reaches the egg and enters it

    (c)   only the acrosome of the sperm enters the egg

    (d)   two haploid nuclei fuse and immediately divide to produce two nuclei, which are again hapiold

(ii) In human beings, the fertilization occurs in the

    (a)   uterus   (b)   ovaries

    (c)   fallopian tubes   (d)   vagina

(iii) The embryo in humans gets nutrition from the mother's blood with the help of a special tissue called

    (a)   Placenta   (b)   Villi

    (c)   Uterus   (d)   Womb

(iv) The ability to reproduce is lost in a female after

    (a)   fertilisation   (b)   menstruation

    (c)   gamcte formation   (d)   mcnopausc

(v) When a sperm is deposited into the vagina which route does it travel?

    (a)   Vagina → Oviduct → Uterus → Cervix   (b)   Vagina → Ovary → Uterus → Oviduct

    (c)   Vagina → Cervix → Uterus → Oviduct   (d)   Vagina → Uterus → Cervix → Oviduct

34. Read the following and attempt any four questions from 34 (i) to 34 (v).

Periodic table is a chart of elements prepared in such a way that elements having similar properties occur in same vertical groups. According to Doberiner's Law of Triads, "in certain triads of three elements the atomic mass of the central element was the arithmetic mean of the atomic masses of the other two elements." But in some triads all the threc elements possessed nearly the same atomic masses, therefore the law was rejected. According to Newland's Law of Octaves "the elements are arranged in such a way that the eighth element starting from a given one has properties which are a repetition of those of the first if arranged in order of increasing atomic weight like the. eight note of musical scale."According to Mendeleev's periodic law, Properties of elements are periodic functions of their atomic masses.In this, there are seven periods and eight groups. Out of 8 groups, seven are of normal elements and one of transition elements.He left gaps in his table for unknown elements. He thought that when these elements would be discovered later on, they could be placed in the table without disturbing other elements.

(i) Upto which element, the Law of Octaves was found to be applicable

    (a) Oxygen   (b) Calcium

    (c) Cobalt   (d) Potassium

(ii) According to Mendeleev's? Periodic Law, the elements were arranged in the periodic table in the order of

    (a) increasing atomic number   (b) decreasing atomic number

    (c) increasing atomic masses   (d) decreasing atomic masses

(iii) In Mendeleev's Periodic Table, gaps were left for the elements to be discovered later. Which of the following elements found a place in the perioidc table later

    (a) Germanium   (b) Chlorine

    (c) Oxgen   (d) Silicon

(iv) What type of oxide would Eka- aluminium form?

    (a) EO_3 (b) E_3O_2

    (c) E_2O_3 (d) EO

(v) Three elements B, Si and Ge are

    (a) metals   (b) non-metals

    (c) metalloids   (d) metal, non-metal and metalloid respectively

35. **Read the following and answer any four questions from 35(i) to 35(v).**

Indicators are chemical compounds that tell us whether a substance is acidic or basic by changing its colour. When added to an acidic solution or a basic solution, indicators change their colour and this change in colour is different for the acids and bases. The indicator thus help us to decide whether a given solution is acidic or basic in nature. The indicators that are obtained from plants are known as natural indicators.Examples - Turmeric, china rosa, red cabbage and grape juice. Some flowers such as the hydrangeas can also determine whether a substance is acidic or basic. Hydrangeas turn blue if the soil is acidic, purple if the soil is neutral and pink if the soil is basic. The colour intensity depends on the amount of acid and base present in the soil.

(i) 'Litmus', a natural dye is an extract of which of the following?

    (a) China rose (Gudhal)   (b) Beetroot

    (c) Lichen   (d) Blue berries (Jamun)

(ii) Phenolphthalein is a synthetic indicator and its colours in acidic and basic solutions, respectively are

    (a) red and blue.   (b) blue and red.

    (c) pink and colourless.   (d) colourless and pink

(iii) When the soil is basic, plants do not grow well in it. To improve its quality what must be added to the soil?

(a) Organic matter (b) Quick lime

(c) Slaked lime (d) Calamine solution

(iv) A solution changes the colour of turmetic indicator from yellow to red. The solution is

(a) basic (b) acidic

(c) neutral (d) either neutral or acidic

(v) Which of the following is an acid-base indicator?

(a) Vinegar (b) Lime water

(c) Turmeric (d) Baking soda

36. Read the following and answer any four questions from 36 (i) to 36 (v).

The space around a magnet (or a current carrying conductor) in which its magnetic effect can be experienced is called the magnetic field. It is a quantity that has both direction and magnitude. The magnetic field in a region is said to be uniform if the magnitude of its strength and direction is same at all points in that region. The strength of magnetic field is also known as magnetic induction or magnetic flux density.

The SI unit of strength of magnetic field is tesla (T)

(i) Which of the following correctly describes the magnetic field near a long straight wire?

(a) The field consists of straight lines perpendicular to the wire.

(b) The field consists of straight lines parallel to the wire.

(c) The field consists of radial lines originating from the wire.

(d) The field consists of concentric circles centred on the wire.

(ii) Which of the following can produce a magnetic field?

(a) Electric charges at rest

(b) Electric charges in motion

(c) Only by permanent magnets

(d) Electric charges whether at rest or in motion

(iii) Choose the incorrect statement from the following regarding magnetic lines of field

(a) The direction of magnetic field at a point is taken to be the direction in which the North pole of a magnetic compass needle points

(b) Magnetic field lines are closed curves

(c) If magnetic field lines are parallel and equidistant, they represent zero field strength

(d) Relative strength of magnetic field is shown by the degree of closeness of the field lines

(iv) Which of the following is a source of magnetic field?

(a) A natural magnet (b) A current carrying conductor

(c) A solenoid (d) All of the above

(v) Which one of the statement best describes the nature of the field lines due to a bar magnet?

    (a)   Field lines start from the north pole and end on the south pole. Any number of field lines can pass through a point.

    (b)   Field lines start from the north pole and end on the south pole. Only one field line passes through a point.

    (c)   Field lines are continuous lines passing inside and outside the magnet. Only one field line passes through a point.

    (d)   Field lines are continuous lines passing inside and outside the magnet. Any number of field lines can pass through a point.

Directions: Q. No. 37-40 contain five sub-parts each. You are expected to answer **any four** sub-parts in these questions.

---

37. **Read the following and answer any four questions from 37(i) to 37(v).**

Acids and bases react to form salt and water. The reaction is known as neutralization reaction. Salts having the same positive or negative radicals are said to belong to a family. For example, $NaCl$ and Na_2SO_4 belong to the family of sodium salts. Similarly, $NaCl$ and KCl belong to the family of chloride salts. The common salt is an important raw material for various materials of daily use, such as sodium hydroxide, baking soda, washing soda, bleaching powder. Bleaching powder is represented as $CaOCl_2$, Bleaching powder is produced by the action of chlorine on dry slaked lime.

(i) Which of the following is 'quicklime'?

    (a) CaO (b) $Ca(OH)_2$ (c)$CaCO_3$ (d) $CaCl_2.6H_2O$

(ii) Select the reaction that is called *'slaking of lime'*

    (a) $CaCO_3 \longrightarrow CaO + CO_2$

    (b) $CaO + 2HCl \longrightarrow CaCl_2 + H_2O$

    (c) $CaCO_3 + H_2O \longrightarrow Ca(OH)_2 + CO_2$

    (d) $CaO + H_2O \longrightarrow Ca(OH)_2$

(iii) Which of the following pairs of substances are chemically same?

    (a) Lime water and milk of lime   (b) Dead burnt plaster and gypsum

    (c) Both the above   (d) None of the above is correct

(iv) The chemical name of bleaching powder is

    (a) calcium chloride   (b) calcium oxychloride

    (c) calcium chloroxide   (d) none of these

(v) Temporary hardness in water is due to which of one the following calcium and magnesium?

    (a) Hydrogen Carbonate   (b) Carbonates

    (c) Chlorides   (d) Sulphates

38. **Read the following and attempt any four questions from 38(i) to 38(v).**

The reproductive parts of angiosperms are located in the flower. The different parts of a flower - sepals, petals, stamens and carpels. Stamens and carpels are the reproductive parts of a flower which contain the germ-cells. The flower may be unisexual (papaya, watermelon) when it contains either stamens or carpels or bisexual (Hibiscus, mustard) when it contains both stamens and carpels. Stamen is the male reproductive part and it produces pollen grains that are yellowish in colour. Carpel is present in the centre of a flower and is the female reproductive part. It is made of three parts. The swollen bottom part is the ovary, middle elongated part is the style and the terminal part which may be sticky is the stigma. The ovary contains ovules and each ovule has an egg cell. The male germ-cell produced by pollen grain fuses with the female gamete present in the ovule. This fusion of the germ-cells or fertilisation gives us the zygote which is capable of growing into a new plant. Thus the pollen needs to be transferred from the stamen to the stigma. If this transfer of pollen occurs in the same flower, it is referred to as self-pollination. On the other hand, if the pollen is transferred from one flower to another, it is known as crosspollination. This transfer of pollen from one flower to another is achieved by agents like wind, water or animals. After the pollen lands on a suitable stigma, it has to reach the female germ-cells which are in the ovary. For this, a tube grows out of the pollen grain and travels through the style to reach the ovary. After fertilisation, the zygote divides several times to form an embryo within the ovule. The ovule develops a tough coat and is gradually converted into a seed. The seed contains the future plant or embryo which develops into a seedling under appropriate conditions. This process is known as germination.

(i) Flower with both androecium and gynoecium and gynoecium are called

  (a) Bisexual flowers   (b) Anther   (c) Stamens   (d) Unisexual flowers

(ii) The process of formation of seeds without fertilization in flowering plants is known as

  (a) Budding   (b) Apomixis   (c) Sporulation   (d) Somatic hybridization

(iii) Which of the following is similar to autogamy, but requires pollinators?

  (a) Geitonogamy   (b) Cleistogamy   (c) Apogamy   (d) Xenogamy

(iv) The stalk of Datura flower at its base is known as

  (a) Pedicel   (b) Corolla   (c) Sepals   (d) Thalamus

(v) The transfer of pollen from the anther to stigma is called

  (a) Pollination   (b) Fertilization   (c) Adoption   (d) Diffusion

39. **Read the following and attempt any four questions from 39(i) to 39(v).**

Electric potential at a point in electric field is defined to be equal to the minimum work done by an external agent in moving a unit positive charge from infinity or a reference point to that point against the electrical force of the field.

Electric potential at a point in electric field is numerically equal but opposite in sign to the work performed by electrical force to bring unit positive charge from infinity to that point.

If W is the work done by external agent in bringing a positive test charge q_0 from infinity to a point then the potential V at that point,

$$V = \frac{W_{ext}}{q_0} \; ;$$

$$V = -\frac{W_E(\text{work done by electric field})}{q_0}$$

The SI unit of electric potential is joule/coulomb or volt.

(i) Volt is the unit of

 (a) emf (b) current (c) resistance (d) charge

(ii) How much energy is given to each coulomb of charge passing through a 6V battery?

 (a) 4 Joule (b) 6 Joule (c) 8 Joule (d) 10 Joule

(iii) Name the device which helps to maintain potential difference across a conductor.

 (a) Ammeter (b) Voltmeter (c) Cell (d) Rheostat

(iv) Name the device which is used to measure the current in the circuit.

 (a) Voltmeter (b) Ammeter (c) Cell (d) Rheostat

(v) In an electric field, the work done in bringing a coulomb charge from infinity to a point A is 10 Joules and in bringing the same charge to some other point B is 20 Joules. Find the potential difference between two points A and B

 (a) 15 V (b) 10 V (c) 5 V (d) 0 V

40. **Read the following and attempt any four questions from 40(i) to 40(v).**

In the early 1800s, the only current producing devices were voltaic cells, which produced small currents by dissolving metals in acids. These were the forerunners of our present-day batteries. The question arose as to whether electricity could be produced from magnetism. The answer was provided in 1831 by two physicists, Michael Faraday in England and Joseph Henry in the United States each working without knowledge of the other. Their discovery changed the world by making electricity common place powering industries by day and lighting up cities at night.

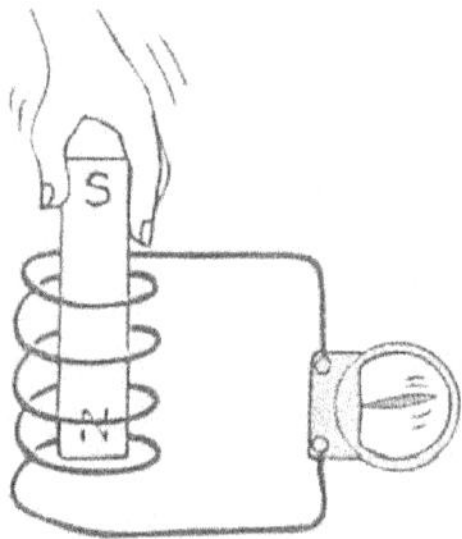

Faraday and Henry both discovered that electric current could be produced in a wire simply by moving a magnet into or out of a coil of wire. No battery or other voltage source was needed only the motion of a magnet in a wire loop. They discovered that voltage is caused, or induced, by the relative motion between a wire and a magnetic field. Whether the magnetic field moves near a stationary conductor or vice versa, voltage is induced either way.

(i) The phenomenon of electromagnetic induction is

 (a) the process of charging a body.

 (b) the process of generating magnetic field due to a current passing through a coil.

 (c) producing induced current in a coil due to relative motion between a magnet and the coil.

 (d) the process of rotating a coil of an electric motor.

(ii) Three rings P, Q and R are dropped at the same time over identical hollow magnets as shown below:

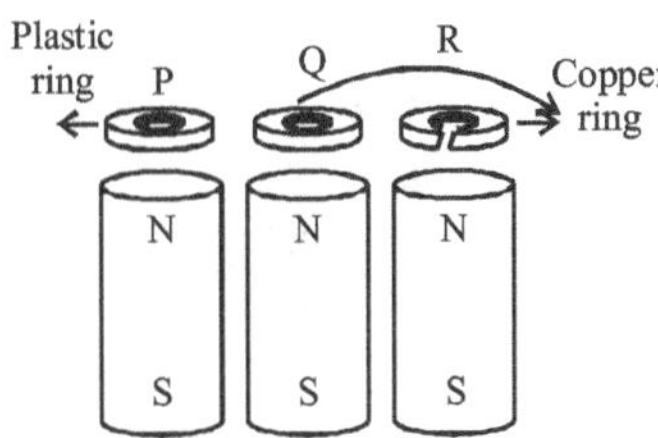

Which of the following describes the order in which the ring P, Q and R reach the bottom of the magnet?

(a)   They arrive in the order P, Q, R.

(b)   They arrive in the order P, R, Q.

(c)   Rings P and R arrive simultaneously, followed by Q.

(d)   Rings Q and R arrive simultaneously, followed by P.

(iii) In the arrangement shown in figure, there are two coils wound on a non-conducting cylindrical rod. Initially, the key is not inserted. Then the key is inserted and later removed. Then

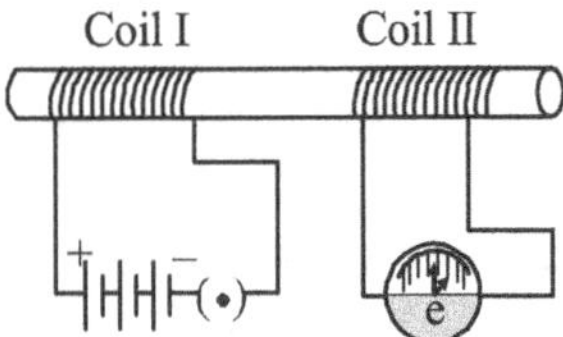

(a)   the deflection in the galvanometer remains zero throughout

(b)   there is a momentary deflection in the golvanometer but it dies out shortly and there is no effect when the key is removed.

(c)   there are momentary galvanometer deflections that die out shortly, the deflections are in the same direction.

(d)   there are momentary galvanometer deflections that die out shortly, the deflections are in opposite directions. Thus the galvanometer shows momentary deflections in opposite directions.

(iv) In the phenomenon of electromagnetic induction, __________ energy of the coil or magnet is converted to __________ energy.

(a)   magnetic, kinetic   (b)   electric, magnetic

(c)   electric, kinetic   (d)   kinetic, electric

(v) A coil is moved towards a stationary magnet. The voltage induced in the coil depends on

(a)   area of the coil

(b)   the speed with which coil is moved towards the bar magnet

(c)   number of turns of the coil

(d)   All of the above

Directions: Q. No. 41-44 contain five sub-parts each. You are expected to answer **any four** sub-parts in these questions.

41. **Read the following and answer any four questions from 41(i) to 41(v).**
acid-base indicators are used to distinguish between an acid and a base. universal indicator is a mixture of several indicators which shows different colours at different concentrations of hydrogen ions in a solution. A scale for measuring hydrogen ion concentration in a solution, called pH scale has been developed. The p in pH stands for 'potenz' in German, meaning power. pH should be thought of simply as a number which indicates the acidic or basic nature of a solution. Higher the hydronium ion concentration, lower is the pH value.

(i) The colour of pH paper when put in distilled water changed to green. Now some common salt is added to water and pH paper is tested in this solution. The colour of pH paper in this case is likely to be
(a) green   (b) yellow   (c) red   (d) blue

(ii) Which natural indicator (acid-base) is used in kitchens of our homes?
(a) Sodium chloride   (b) Tea leaves
(c) Sodium carbonate   (d) Turmeric

(iii) A drop of liquid sample was put on pH paper. The colour of pH paper turned blue. The liquid sample could be
(a) lemon juice   (b) hydrochloric acid
(c) sodium hydrogen carbonate   (d) ethanoic acid.

(iv) Universal indicator solution is named as such because
(a) it is available universally   (b) it has a universal appearance
(c) it can be used for entire pH range   (d) All the above are correct

(v) An indicator that turns reddish-brown when dissolved in soap solution is
(a) litmus   (b) china rose
(c) turmeric powder   (d) None of these

42. **Read the following and attempt any four questions from 42 (i) to 42 (v).**
The blood being a fluid connective tissue. Blood consists of fluid medium called plasma in which the cells are suspended. Plasma transports food, carbon dioxide and nitrogenous wastes in dissolved form. Oxygen is carried by the red blood cells. Many other substances like salts are also transported by the blood. There is another type of fluid also involved in transportation. This is called lymph or tissue fluid. Through the pores present in the walls of capillaries some amount of plasma, proteins and blood cells escape into intercellular spaces in the tissues to form the tissue fluid or lymph. It is similar to the plasma of blood but colourless and contains less protein. Lymph drains into lymphatic capillaries from the intercellular spaces, which join to form large lymph vessels that finally open into larger veins. Lymph carries digested and absorbed fat from intestine and drains excess fluid from extra cellular space back into the blood.

(i) ------- forms clots when blood vessels get damaged.
(a) Platelets   (b) Cellulose   (c) Haemoglobin   (d) None of the above

(ii) ------- is a fluid that drains from the lacteals of the small intestine into the lymphatic system during digestion. It usually contains fat and proteins.
(a) Chyme   (b) Bile   (c) Chyle   (d) None of the above

(iii) ------- is a small branch of an artery that leads into a capillary.
(a) Capillaria   (b) Areolas   (c) Arteriole   (d) None of the above

(iv) Lymph is without
(a) Leucocytes   (b) Plasma   (c) Erythrocytes   (d) None of the above

(v) Blood does not contain
(a) Calcium   (b) Prothrombin   (c) Fibrinoge   (d) Elastin

43. **Read the following and attempt any four questions from 43(i) to 43(v).**

We know that when light goes from one medium to another medium having different optical densities, then refraction of light rays (or bending of light rays) takes place. Now, in the atmosphere, we have air everywhere. But all the air in the atmosphere is not at the same temperature. Some of the air layers of the atmosphere are cold whereas other air layers of the atmosphere are comparatively warm (or hotter). Now the cooler air layers of the atmosphere behave as optically denser medium for light rays whereas the warmer air layers (or hotter air layers) of the atmosphere behave as optically rarer medium for the light rays. So, in the same atmosphere we have air layers having different optical densities. And when light rays pass through the atmosphere having air layers of different optical densities, then refraction of light takes place. The refraction of light caused by the earth's atmosphere (having air layers of varying optical densities) is called atmospheric refraction.

(i) With respect to atmospheric refraction which of the following point distinguish between cold air and hot air?

    (a) Cold air is denser than hot air   (b) Hot air is lighter than cold air

    (c) Cold air has higher refractive   (d) All of these

(ii) What is the reason behind twinkling of stars?

    (a) Dispersion of star light   (b) Reflection of star light

    (c) Refraction of star light   (d) All of these

(iii) Why sun appears flattened during sunrise and sunset?

    (a) Because sun is closer to earth   (b) Because earth is rotating

    (c) Because earth is revolving   (d) Because of atmospheric refraction

(iv) How much time from sunrise to sunset is lengthened because of atmospheric refraction

    (a) 4 hours   (b) 2 minutes   (c) 4 minutes   (d) 2 hours

(v) When light rays from stars enter into earth's atmosphere, it travels from

    (a) Denser to rarer medium   (b) Rarer to denser medium

    (c) Rarer medium to vocuum   (d) Denser medium to vacuum

44. **Read the following and attempt any four questions from 44 (i) to 44 (v).**

A solenoid is a long cylindrical helix. It is made by winding closely a large number of turns of insulated copper wire over a tube of card-board or china-clay. When electric current is passed through the solenoid, a magnetic field is produced around and within the solenoid.

(i) The magnetic field strength of a solenoid can be increased by inserting which of the following materials as a corc?

    (a) Gold   (b) Silver   (c) Iron   (d) Aluminium

(ii) What happens to the magnetic field in the solenoid when the current increases?

    (a) Increase   (b) Decreases   (c) Remains constant   (d) Becomes zero

(iii) What is the magnetic filed outside the solenoid?

    (a) Infinity   (b) Zero

    (c) Double the value of the field inside   (d) Half the value of field inside

(iv) What happens to the magnetic field when number of turns of the solenoid increases?

    (a) Increases   (b) Decreases   (c) Remains constant   (d) Becomes infinity

(v) The magnetic field inside a long strainght solenoid carrying current

    (a) is zero   (b) decreases as we move towards the end

    (c) increases as we move towards the end   (d) is the same at all points

Case Study Based MCQs Solution

1. (i)   (b)   Tissue respiration
    (ii) (b)   Anaerobic respiration
    (iii) (b)

Aerobic	Anaerobic	Amount of energy is high and consistent in aerobic and low in anaerobic

    (iv) (c)   (ii), (iii), (iv) only
    (v)   (a)   Location Aerobic-Cyloplasm and Anaerobic-Mitochondria
2. (i)   (c) $Cs > Rb > K > Na > Li$
    (ii) (b)   As Hydrogen can easily lose one electrion like alkali metals to form positive ion
    (iii) (a)   F
    (iv) (c)   Electronegativity decreases down the group due to increase in atomic radius/ tendency to gain election decreases.
    (v)   (d)   F and Li are in the same period and across the period atomic size/radius decreases from left to right.
3. (i)   (b)   Convex

    (ii) (b) $P = \dfrac{1}{f}$

    $$P_1 = \frac{1}{f_1} \text{ and } P_2 = \frac{1}{f_2}$$

    $$P_1 = P_2 = \frac{4}{1}, \text{ hence } \frac{\left(\dfrac{1}{f_1}\right)}{\left(\dfrac{1}{f_2}\right)} = \frac{4}{1}$$

    $$\text{Hence } \frac{f_1}{f_2} = \frac{1}{4}$$

    (iii) (a)   Ratio of height of image to height of object

    (iv) (c) $m = \dfrac{v}{u}$

    $$3 = \frac{24}{u}$$

    Hence $u = 8$ cm
    (v)   (e)   Not-so-thick lenses would not make the telescope very heavy and they will also allow considerable amount of light to pass through them.
4. (i)   (c)   Electrical to Mechanical
    (ii) (b)   The bar will be magnetised as long as there is current in the circuit.
    (iii) (a)   A bar magnet

    (iv) (d) Only II

    (v) (a) For a current of 0.8 A the magnetic field is 13 mT

5. (i) (a) carbon compounds are covalent compounds.

    (ii) (b) carbon compounds are generally covalent compounds therefore they have lower melting and boiling points than ionic compounds.

    (iii) (a) Glacial acetic acid is pure acetic acid free of water.

    (iv) (b) although graphite has covalent bonding it is a good conductor of electricity due to the presence of free electron.

    (v) (b) covalent bond is weaker than ionic bond.

6. (i) (b),   (ii) (d),   (iii) (c),   (iv) (b),   (v) (a)

7. (i) (a) From figure, angle of incidence, $i = 60°$ and angle of refraction, $r = 45°$

Refractive index of the medium B relative to medium A, (from Snell's law)

$$\mu_{BA} = \frac{\sin i}{\sin r} = \frac{\sin 60°}{\sin 45°} = \frac{\left(\dfrac{\sqrt{3}}{2}\right)}{\left(\dfrac{1}{\sqrt{2}}\right)} = \frac{\sqrt{3}}{2}$$

    (ii) (a) Since light rays in the medium B goes towards normal (figure), so it has greater refractive index i.e., denser w.r.t. medium A. Hence, refractive index of medium B relative to medium A is greater than unity.

    (iii) (b) In a rectangular glass slab, the emergent rays are parallel to the direction of the incident ray, as the extent of bending of the ray of light at the opposite parallel faces air-glass and glass-air interface of the rectangular glass slab is equal and opposite.

This is why the ray emerges are parallel to the incident ray.

    (iv) (d) Among the given material kerosene refractive index, $\mu = 1.44$, water $\mu = 1.33$, mustard oil $\mu = 1.46$ and glycerine $\mu = 1.74$. Glycerine is most optically denser. Therefore, ray of light bend most in glycerine.

    (v) (a) $\dfrac{\sin i}{\sin r} = n_{21} = \dfrac{v_1}{v_2}$

8. (i) (a) Three oxygen utoms

    (ii) (b) ultraviolet (UV) radiation

    (iii) (c) 1980s

    (iv) (d) 1986

    (v) (a) Skin cancer

9. (i) (b),   (ii) (a),   (iii) (d),   (iv) (a),   (v) (b)

10. (i) (d) The maximum resistance is obtained when resistors are connected in series. Thus equivalent resistance

$$R_{eq} = n \times R = 5 \times \frac{1}{5} = 1\,\Omega$$

R_{eq} = equired equivalent resistance for series combination.

    (ii) (b) The minimum resistance is obtained when resistors are connected in parallel combination. Thus, equivalent resistance,

$$R' = \frac{R}{n} = \frac{1/5}{5} = \frac{1}{25}\,\Omega,$$

R' = required equivalent resistance for parallel combination.

(iii) (c) We know that, $R = \rho \dfrac{l}{A}$

where, ρ = resistivity, l = length, A = area.
For first and second conductor,

$$R_1 = \dfrac{\rho_1 l_1}{A_1}, \; R_2 = \dfrac{\rho_2 l_2}{A_2}$$

$$\dfrac{R_1}{R_2} = \dfrac{\rho_1}{\rho_2} \dfrac{l_1}{l_2} \times \dfrac{A_2}{A_1} \Rightarrow \dfrac{R}{R} = \dfrac{\rho}{\rho} \times \dfrac{l}{2l} \times \dfrac{A_2}{A} \Rightarrow A_2 = 2A \; [\text{as given } R_1 = R_2 = R, l_1 = l, l_2 = 2l,$$

$$\rho_1 = \rho_2 = \rho \text{ (same material)]}$$

(iv) (b) As we know that in series combination of resistances same current flows through each resistor where as in parallel combination same voltage exist across each resistor.

(v) (d) Now, resistance of each wire is R/5.

Equivalent resistance is given by $\dfrac{1}{R'} = \dfrac{5}{R} + \dfrac{5}{R} + \dfrac{5}{R} + \dfrac{5}{R} + \dfrac{5}{R} = \dfrac{25}{R}$

$$\Rightarrow \dfrac{R}{R'} = 25$$

11. (i) (a) R and Q are members of Group 16th which is non metallic having O, S, Se, Te etc. RQ_2 is characterised by showing the formation of covalent bond.

(ii) (c) G

(iii) (d) Element 'V' is the most electronegative element.

(iv) (b) J shows +2 oxidation in its compounds.

(v) (c) V shows −1 oxidation state.

12. (i) (b), (ii) (a), (iii) (d), (iv) (c), (v) (a)

13. (i) (a) Convex lens

(ii) (a) A parallel beam of sun rays get converged by a convex lens as a sharp, bright spot. This is the real image of the sun.

(iii) (c)

(iv) (a) A ray parallel to principal axis must pass through focus and a ray passing through focus must go parallel to principal axis.

(v) (a) Here, ray of light passing through principal focus of the lens. A ray of light passing through the principal focus of a convex lens after refraction will emerge parallel to the principal axis.

14. (i) (b)

(ii) (c) Sodium hydroxide being a base neturalises the acid.

(iii) (b) Alkali is a base which are water soluble.

(iv) (d)

(v) (a) Na_2CO_3 is formed from NaOH and H_2CO_3 i.e, strong base and weak acid.

15. (i) (a) As metals are electropositive in nature and have tendency to lose electrons.

(ii) (c)

(iii) (b) It is because of extremely high reactivity of sodium.

(iv) (c) In chloroplast Mg is present.

(v) (d) Sodium and potassium both are extremely reactive and react with water so vigorously. This reaction is highly exothermic so that hydrogen evolved will catch fire.

16. (i) (c) (ii) (b) (iii) (b) (iv) (d) (v) (b)

17. (i) (d) Fleming's right hand rule.

(ii) (d) Velocity and force change due to change in direction but magnitude of PE and KE of electron remain constant speed is constant.

(iii) (b) Magnetic field (B) is produced by moving charge.

(iv) (b) According to Fleming's left hand rule the direction of force on the wire will be down into the page.

(v) (c) A long coil of finite length of wire carrying current consisting of closely packed loops is called solenoid whose magnetic field resembles that of a bar magnet.

18. (i) (d) Ga has very low m.pt.

(ii) (d)

(iii) (c) As silver is less reactive in nature it will not displace hydrogen from dilute acids.

(iv) (d) $Zn + H_2O \text{ (Steam)} \longrightarrow ZnO + H_2$

(v) (c)

19. (i) (a)

(ii) (d) Size of F^- less than O^{2-}.

(iii) (b)

(iv) (b)

K L M
2 8 6

The element has more than 4 valence electron, it is a non-metal. It is short of two electrons to attain nearest noble gas configurations hence, its valency is 2.

(v) (c)

20. (i) (b) (ii) (a) (iii) (b) (iv) (b) (v) (c)

21. (i) (b) (ii) (a) (iii) (d) (iv) (a) (v) (d)

22. (i) (b) Generally, in case of a prism (i), the formation of spectrum is shown below

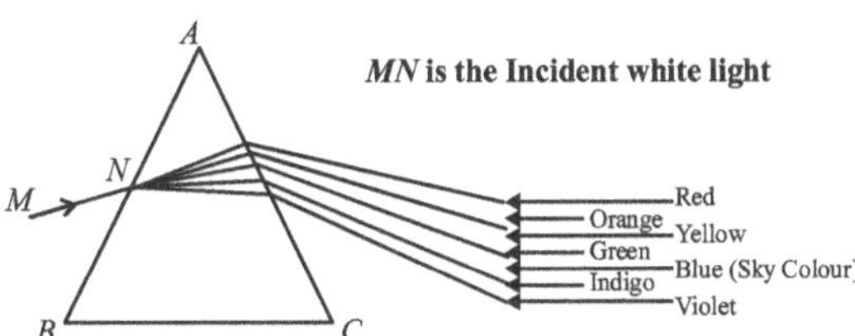

In the above figure, from top the third colour is yellow. But we can see that from bottom the third colour is blue (colour of sky). So, we can obtain the correct situation by inverting the prism. Thus the required orientations can be found in case (ii).

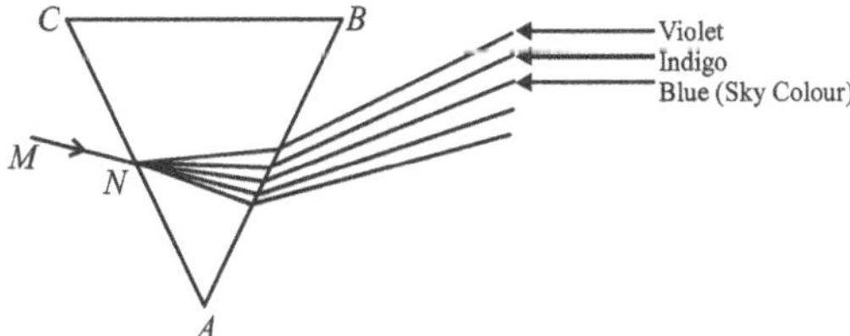

So, option (b) is correct.

(ii) (c) Speed of light is same for all colours of white light in air but different colours have different wavelengths and frequencies.

(iii) (b) Red

(iv) (d) Violet

(v) (d) Violet

23. (i) (b)

(ii) (d) It is an example of displacement reaction. In it Al metal displaces iron from Fe_2O_3 when reaction is carried out in aqueous solution.

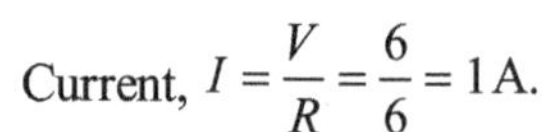

(iii) (c) a. $Mg + CuO \longrightarrow MgO + Cu$

b. Copper is displaced by Mg.

(iv) (d) As in all above reactions complex substances decomposes to give simple subtances.

(v) (a) As here H_2 gets oxidised and CuO reduced to Cu.

24. (i) (d), (ii) (c), (iii) (d), (iv) (a), (v) (b)

25. (i) (b) $P = VI = V^2/R = I^2R$

(ii) (d) $P = \dfrac{V^2}{R} \Rightarrow R = \dfrac{V^2}{P} = \dfrac{220 \times 220}{100} = 484\ \Omega$

$P = \dfrac{V^2}{R} = \dfrac{110 \times 110}{484} = 25\,W$

(iii) (c) $R_S = R_1 + R_2 = R + R = 2R$

$\dfrac{1}{R_P} = \dfrac{1}{R_1} + \dfrac{1}{R_2} = \dfrac{1}{R} + \dfrac{1}{R} = \dfrac{2}{R}$

$R_P = R/2$

$\dfrac{H_1}{H_2} = \dfrac{V^2}{R_S}\dfrac{R_P}{V^2} = \dfrac{R_P}{R_S} = \dfrac{R}{2 \times 2R} = \dfrac{1}{4} = 1:4.$

(iv) (c) The bulb with the highest wattage glows with maximum brightness. Brightness of bulb B (100 W) is maximum.

Correct order of brightness will be,

Bulb of 100 W > Bulb of 60 W > Bulb of 40 W.

(v) (c) Given, resistors, $R_1 = 2\Omega$ and $R_2 = 4\Omega$

Voltgage, $V = 6\,V$

Equivalent Resistance,

$= R_1 + R_2 = 2 + 4 = 6\Omega$ [Series combination]

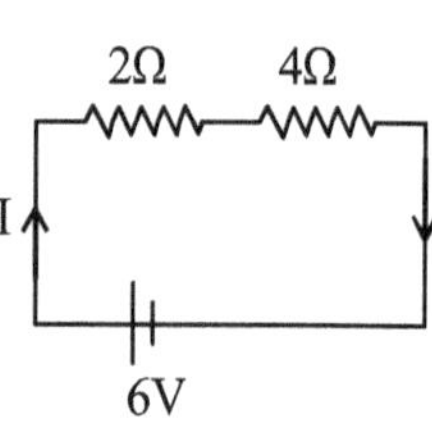

Current, $I = \dfrac{V}{R} = \dfrac{6}{6} = 1\,A.$

Heat dissipated in 4Ω Resistor

$= I^2Rt = 1 \times 4 \times 5 = 20\,J$ $[\because I = 1A, R = 4\Omega, t = 5\ \text{sec.}]$

26. (i) (a) The sun appears white as little of the blue and violet colours are scattered. At noon light from the sun is directly over head and travel relatively shorter distance.

(ii) (b) Scattering $\alpha \dfrac{1}{\lambda^4}$

(iii) (c) The clear sky appears blue because the molecules in the air scatter blue light (smaller wavelength) from the sun more than they scatter other colour (larger wavelength).

(iv) (b) Scattering $\alpha \dfrac{1}{\lambda^4}$

(v) (c) The colour of water in deep sea looks blue because the red, green, orange and yellow having longer wavelengths are absorbed more strongly by water than blue which has shorter wavelength. So, when white light from the sun enters the sea, it is mostly the blue that gets returned, while other colours absorbed. Also, blue coloured light is scattered more by fine particles in water.

27. (i) (a) Alveoli
(ii) (c) Mediastinum
(iii) (d) All of the above
(iv) (a) Alveoli
(v) (b) External respiration

28. (i) (d) Due to presence of different functional groups methyl alcohol and acetic acid. Possess different physical and chemical properties.

(ii) (c)
(iii) (d) Butane and isobutane have same chemical formula but different arrangement of atoms and have different structure.

$$
\begin{array}{cccc}
\text{H} & \text{H} & \text{H} & \text{H} \\
| & | & | & | \\
\text{H}-\text{C}-\text{C}-\text{C}-\text{C}-\text{H} \\
| & | & | & | \\
\text{H} & \text{H} & \text{H} & \text{H}
\end{array}
\quad , \quad
\begin{array}{ccc}
\text{H} & \text{H} & \text{H} \\
| & | & | \\
\text{H}-\text{C}-\text{C}-\text{C}-\text{H} \\
| & | & | \\
\text{H} & \text{H}-\text{C}-\text{H} & \text{H} \\
& | & \\
& \text{H} &
\end{array}
$$

(Butane) (Isobutane)

(iv) (d) Carborundum is SiC (silicon carbide).

$$
\begin{array}{ccccc}
\text{H} & \text{H} & \text{H} & \text{H} & \text{H} \\
| & | & | & | & | \\
\text{H}-\text{C}-\text{C}-\text{C}-\text{C}-\text{C}-\text{H} \\
| & | & | & | & | \\
\text{H} & \text{H} & \text{H} & \text{H} & \text{H}
\end{array}
$$

(v) (c) pentane

29. (i) (b) If a gene is heterozygous it will have two different alleles for the same gene, thus in case of monohybrid cross where only a single gene is considered maximum two alleles are under consideration. For dihybrid cross the number will be 4.

(ii) (c) In the case of incomplete dominance the phenotype of the heterozygote is intermediate to that of the homozygote in both recessive and dominant cases. Then the ratio of both genotype and phenotype is 1:2:1.

(iii) (b) In this case tall in the dominant trait. Then all the F1 progeny will be heterozygotes where the dominant phenotype tall is expressed.

(iv) (d)

(v) (c)

30. (i) (d) Because of the presence of same number of valence electrons the elements of same group have similar chemical properties.

(ii) (d) In group 13, boron is above aluminium. Rest of elements do not belong to group 13.

(iii) (b) Anion O^{2-} has 10 electrons.
Anion F^- has 10 electrons.

(iv) (b) A family of elements consists of elements present in a group of the periodic table.

(v) (c)

31. (i) (b),   (ii) (d),   (iii) (b),   (iv) (a),   (v) (c)

32. (i) (d) $P = \dfrac{100}{-75} = -\dfrac{4}{3} D$

(ii) (d) Power of a lens, $P = \dfrac{1}{f \text{ (in metre)}}$

Power of combination of lens $= 1.5 = \dfrac{1}{f' \text{ (in metre)}}$

$\therefore f' = \dfrac{1}{1.5}$

And, $\dfrac{1}{F} = \dfrac{1}{f_1} + \dfrac{1}{f_2}$ or, $1.5 = \dfrac{1}{0.5} + \dfrac{1}{f_2}$

$\Rightarrow \dfrac{1}{f_2} = \dfrac{1}{0.5} - 1.5 \therefore f_2 = 2m$

Hence second lens is a convex lens of focal length 2m.

(iii) (a) As we know, power of a lens $P = \dfrac{1}{f}$, where f is the focal length in metre and power in dioptre.

$P = \dfrac{1}{f} \Rightarrow f = \dfrac{1}{P} = \dfrac{1}{4} = 0.25$ m

Power of a convex lens is positive.

(iv) (a) $P = \dfrac{1}{f} \Rightarrow -2 = \dfrac{1}{f} \Rightarrow f = \dfrac{-1}{2} m = -50$ m

The lens is concave lens.

(v) (a) $P = \dfrac{1}{f}$

$\Rightarrow P = \dfrac{-1}{2} = -0.5 D$

33. (i) (a)   (ii) (c)   (iii) (a)   (iv) (d)   (v) (c)
34. (i) (b)   (ii) (c)   (iii) (a)   (iv) (c)   (v) (c)
35. (i) (c)   (ii) (d)   (iii) (a)   (iv) (a)   (v) (c)
36. (i) (d)   The field consists of concentric circles centred on the wire according to Maxwell's Right Hand Grip Rule.

   (ii) (b)   Magnetic field (B) is produced by moving charge.

   (iii) (c)   Consider the diagram given below to represent the magnetic field lines around a bar magnet.

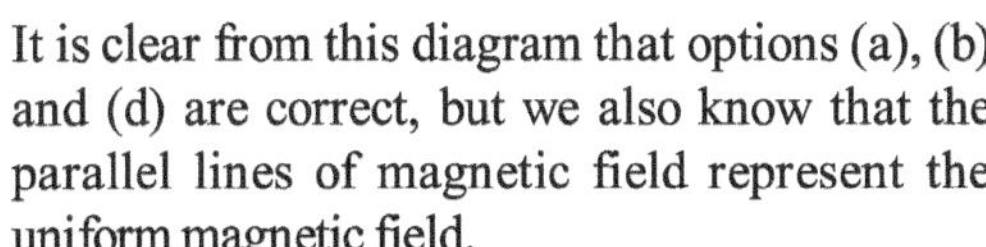

   It is clear from this diagram that options (a), (b) and (d) are correct, but we also know that the parallel lines of magnetic field represent the uniform magnetic field.
   Hence option (c) is incorrect statement.

   (iv) (d)   Magnetic field can be produced by a natural magnet, current carrying conductor and solenoid.

   (v) (d)   Magnetic field lines start from the north pole and end on the south pole outside the magnet and inside the magnet from south to north pole.

37. (i) (a)   (ii) (d)   (iii) (a)   (iv) (b)

   (v) (a)   Temporary hardness in water is due to presence of Hydrogen Carbonate of Ca & Mg.

38. (i) (a)   (ii) (b)   (iii) (a)   (iv) (a)   (v) (a)

39. (i) (a)   Volt is the unit of emf.

   (ii) (b) $W = V \times Q = 6 \times 1 = 6$ Joules

   (iii) (c)   Cell is used to maintain potential difference across a conductor.

   (iv) (b)   Ammeter is used to measure current in the circuit.

   (v) (b)   Potential at point A, $V_A = \dfrac{10J}{1C} = 10V$

   Potential at point B, $V_B = \dfrac{20J}{1C} = 20V$

   Potential difference between A and B = 20V – 10V = 10V

40. (i) (c)   Producing induced current in a coil due to relative motion between a magnet & the coil.

   (ii) (c)   Plastic is non magnetic substance and open ring does not form magnetic poles so due to induction only ring Q will experience retarding force by forming magnetic poles.

   (iii) (d)   In the arrangement shown in the question, when an electric current through the first coil is changed, an emf is induced in the coil due to change in magnetic field lines which pass through the neighbouring second coil.
   The moment when key is inserted and removed, the magnetic field lines passes through second coil increases and decreases in two cases respectively. Therefore, the direction of current in two cases is in opposite directions. So, the galvanometer shows momentary deflections in opposite directions.

   (iv) (d)   In the phenomenon of electromagnetic induction kinetic energy of the coil or magnet is converted to electric energy

   (v) (d)   The voltage induced depends on the number of turns of the coil, the speed with which coil is moved towards the bar magnet and area of the coil.

41. (i) (a) NaCl solution in water is neutral i.e., pH = 7, the same as that of distilled water as NaCl is a salt of strong acid and strong base.

    (ii) (d) Turmeric is an example of natural pH indicator. It can be used to determine acidic or basic character of a substnace.

    (iii) (c) The blue colour of pH paper indicates basic nature of solution. Only sodium hydrogen carbonate solution show basic nature, all others are acidic.

    (iv) (c) It can be for entire pH range.

    (v) (c)

42. (i) (a) Platelets

    (ii) (c) Chyle

    (iii) (c) Arteriole

    (iv) (c) Erythrocytes

    (v) (d) Elastin

43. (i) (a) Cold air is denser than hot air (lighter). Also, cold air has higher refractive index than hot air. Hence, all are true.

    (ii) (c) Twinkling of stars is due to refraction of star light.

    (iii) (d) The sun appears flattened because of atmospheric refraction.

    (iv) (c) The time from sunrise to sunset is lengthened by 4 minutes.

    (v) (b) When light rays from stars enter into earth's atmosphere it travels from rare to denser medium

44. (i) (c) Magnetic field strength can be increased by inserting iron as a core.

    (ii) (a) On increasing current, magnetic field increases.

    (iii) (b) Magnetic field outside the solenoid is zero.

    (iv) (a) On increasing number of turns, magnetic field increases.

    (v) (d) The magnetic field inside the solenoid is same at all points.

Latest Revised Syllabus Issued by CBSE for Academic Year (2020-2021)

Time: 3 Hours   **MATHEMATICS (CODE NO. 041)**   **Max. Marks: 80**

Unit No.	Unit Name	Marks
I	Number Systems	06
II	Algebra	20
III	Coordinate Geometry	06
IV	Geometry	15
V	Trigonometry	12
VI	Mensuration	10
VII	Statistics & Probability	11
	Total	**80**

UNIT I: NUMBER SYSTEMS

1. **Real Number**

    Fundamental Theorem of Arithmetic - statements after reviewing work done earlier and after illustrating and motivating through examples, Proofs of irrationality of $\sqrt{2}, \sqrt{3}, \sqrt{5}$ Decimal representation of rational numbers in terms of terminating/non-terminating recurring decimals.

> ✘ | **Euclid's division lemma**

UNIT II : ALGEBRA

1. **Polynomials**

    Zeros of a polynomial. Relationship between zeros and coefficients of quadratic polynomials.

> ✘ | **Statement and simple problems on division algorithm for polynomials with real coefficients.**

2. **Pair of Linear Equations in Two Variables**

    Pair of linear equations in two variables and graphical method of their solution, consistency/inconsistency.

    Algebraic conditions for number of solutions. Solution of a pair of linear equations in two variables algebraically - by substitution, by elimination. Simple situational problems. Simple problems on equations reducible to linear equations.

> ✘ | **Cross multiplication method**

3. **Quadratic Equations**

    Standard form of a quadratic equation $ax^2 + bx + c = 0$, $(a \neq 0)$. Solutions of quadratic equations (only real roots) by factorization, and by using quadratic formula. Relationship between discriminant and nature of roots.

> ✘ | **Situational problems based on quadratic equations related to day to day activities to be incorporated.**

4. **Arithmetic Progressions**

    Motivation for studying Arithmetic Progression Derivation of the nth term and sum of the first n terms of A.P.

> ✘ | **Application of Arithmetic Progressions in solving daily life problems.**

UNIT III : COORDINATE GEOMETRY

1. **LINES (In two-dimensions)**

    Review: Concepts of coordinate geometry, graphs of linear equations. Distance formula. Section formula (internal division).

> ✘ | **Area of a triangle.**

UNIT IV : GEOMETRY

1. **Triangles**

    Definitions, examples, counter examples of similar triangles.

1. (Prove) If a line is drawn parallel to one side of a triangle to intersect the other two sides in distinct points, the other two sides are divided in the same ratio.
2. (Motivate) If a line divides two sides of a triangle in the same ratio, the line is parallel to the third side.
3. (Motivate) If in two triangles, the corresponding angles are equal, their corresponding sides are proportional and the triangles are similar.
4. (Motivate) If the corresponding sides of two triangles are proportional, their corresponding angles are equal and the two triangles are similar.
5. (Motivate) If one angle of a triangle is equal to one angle of another triangle and the sides including these angles are proportional, the two triangles are similar.
6. (Motivate) If a perpendicular is drawn from the vertex of the right angle of a right triangle to the hypotenuse, the triangles on each side of the perpendicular are similar to the whole triangle and to each other.
7. (Prove) In a right triangle, the square on the hypotenuse is equal to the sum of the squares on the other two sides.

✖	**(Prove) The ratio of the areas of two similar triangles is equal to the ratio of the squares of their corresponding sides.** **(Prove) In a triangle, if the square on one side is equal to sum of the squares on the other two sides, the angles opposite to the first side is a right angle.**

2. **Circles**

Tangent to a circle at, point of contact

1. (Prove) The tangent at any point of a circle is perpendicular to the radius through the point of contact.
2. (Prove) The lengths of tangents drawn from an external point to a circle are equal.

3. **Constructions**

1. Division of a line segment in a given ratio (internally).
2. Tangents to a circle from a point outside it.

✖	**Construction of a triangle similar to a given triangle.**

UNIT V : TRIGONOMETRY

1. **Introduction to Trigonometry**

Trigonometric ratios of an acute angle of a right-angled triangle. Proof of their existence (well defined); Values of the trigonometric ratios of $30°$, $45°$ and $60°$. Relationships between the ratios.

✖	**Motive the ratios whichever are defined at $0°$ and $90°$.**

2. **Trigonometric Identities**

Proof and applications of the identity $\sin^2 A + \cos^2 A = 1$. Only simple identities to be given.

✖	**Trigonometric ratios of complementary angles**

3. **Heights and Distances: Angle of Elevation, Angle of Depression.**

Simple problems on heights and distances. Problems should not involve more than two right triangles. Angles of elevation / depression should be only $30°$, $45°$, $60°$.

UNIT VI : MENSURATION

1. **Areas Related to Circles**

Motivate the area of a circle; area of sectors and segments of a circle. Problems based on areas and perimeter / circumference of the above said plane figures. (In calculating area of segment of a circle, problems should be restricted to central angle of $60°$ and $90°$ and $120°$ only. Plane figures involving triangles, simple quadrilaterals and circle should be taken.)

2. **Surface Areas and Volumes**

1. Surface areas and volumes of combinations of any two of the following: cubes, cuboids, spheres, hemispheres and right circular cylinders/cones.

✖	**Frustum of a cone.**

2. Problems involving converting one type of metallic solid into another and other mixed problems. (Problems with combination of not more than two different solids be taken).

UNIT VII : STATISTICS AND PROBABILITY

1. **Statistics**

Mean, median and mode of grouped data (bimodal situation and step deviation method for finding the mean to be avoided).

✖	**Cumulative frequency graph.**

2. **Probability**

Classical definition of probability. Simple problems on finding the probability of an event.

CBSE Sample Paper 2021

INSTRUCTION: Question 1 to 44 are case based questions. Attempt any 4 sub parts. Each question carry 1 mark.

1. Mathematics teacher of a school took her 10th standard students to show Red fort. It was a part of their Educational trip. The teacher had interest in history as well. She narrated the facts of Red fort to students. Then the teacher said in this monument one can find combination of solid figures. There are 2 pillars which are cylindrical in shape. Also 2 domes at the corners which are hemispherical. 7 smaller domes at the centre. Flag hoisting ceremony on Independence Day takes place near these domes.

   (i) How much cloth material will be required to cover 2 big domes each of radius 2.5 metres?
(Take $\pi = 22/7$)

     (a) $75 m^2$ (b) $78.57 m^2$ (c) $87.47 m^2$ (d) $25.8 m^2$

   (ii) Write the formula to find the volume of a cylindrical pillar.

     (a) $\pi r^2 h$ (b) $\pi r l$ (c) $\pi r(l+r)$ (d) $2\pi r$

   (iii) Find the lateral surface area of two pillars if height of the pillar is 7m and radius of the base is 1.4m.

     (a) $112.3 cm^2$ (b) $123.2 m^2$ (c) $90 m^2$ (d) $345.2 cm^2$

   (iv) How much is the volume of a hemisphere if the radius of the base is 3.5m?

     (a) $85.9 m^3$ (b) $80 m^3$ (c) $98 m^3$ (d) $89.83 m^3$

   (v) What is the ratio of sum of volumes of two hemispheres of radius 1cm each to the volume of a sphere of radius 2 cm?

     (a) $1:1$ (b) $1:8$ (c) $8:1$ (d) $1:16$

2. Class X students of a secondary school in Krishnagar have been allotted a rectangular plot of a land for gardening activity. Saplings of Gulmohar are planted on the boundary at a distance of 1m from each other. There is a triangular grassy lawn in the plot as shown in the fig. The students are to sow seeds of flowering plants on the remaining area of the plot.

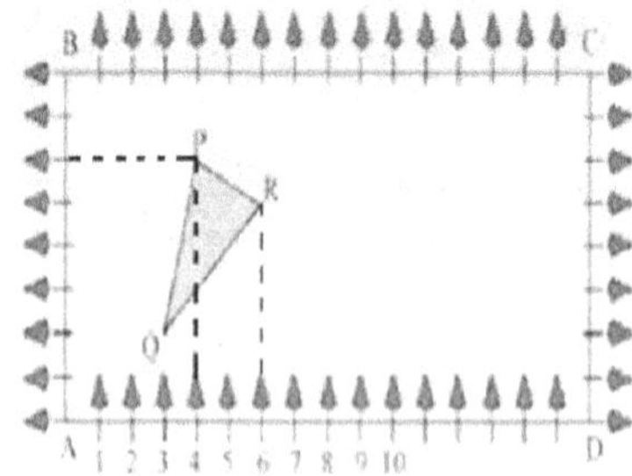

Considering A as origin, answer question (i) to (v)

(i) Considering A as the origin, what are the coordinates of A?

    (a) $(0, 1)$ (b) $(1, 0)$ (c) $(0, 0)$ (d) $(-1, -1)$

(ii) What are the coordinates of P?

    (a) $(4, 6)$ (b) $(6, 4)$ (c) $(4, 5)$ (d) $(5, 4)$

(iii) What are the coordinates of R?

    (a) $(6, 5)$ (b) $(5, 6)$ (c) $(6, 0)$ (d) $(7, 4)$

(iv) What are the coordinates of D?

    (a) $(16, 0)$ (b) $(0, 0)$ (c) $(0, 16)$ (d) $(16, 0)$

(v) What are the coordinate of P if D is taken as the origin?

    (a) $(12, 2)$ (b) $(-12, 2)$ (c) $(12, 3)$ (d) $(6, 10)$

3. Rahul is studying in X Standard. He is making a kite to fly it on a Sunday. Few questions came to his mind while making the kite. Give answers to his questions by looking at the figure.

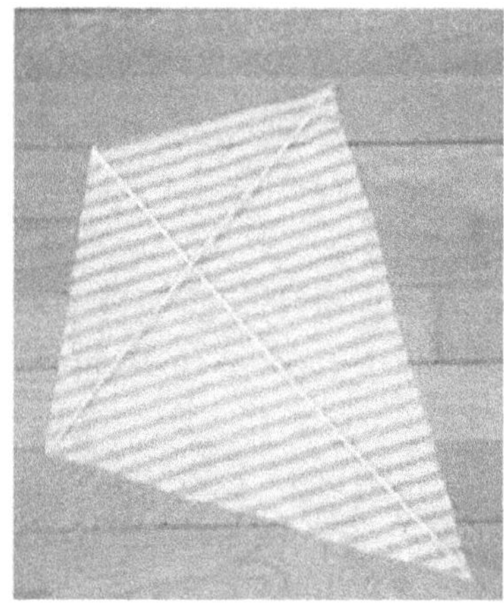

(i) Rahul tied the sticks at what angles to each other?

    (a) $30°$ (b) $60°$ (c) $90°$ (d) $60°$

(ii) Which is the correct similarity criteria applicable for smaller triangles at the upper part of this kite?

    (a) RHS   (b) SAS   (c) SSA   (d) AAS

(iii) Sides of two similar triangles are in the ratio 4:9. Corresponding medians of these triangles are in the ratio,

    (a) $2:3$ (b) $4:9$ (c) $81:16$ (d) $16:81$

(iv) In a triangle, if square of one side is equal to the sum of the squares of the other two sides, then the angle opposite the first side is a right angle. This theorem is called as,

    (a) Pythagoras theorem   (b) Thales theorem

    (c) Converse of Thales theorem   (d) Converse of Pythagoras theorem

(v) What is the area of the kite, formed by two perpendicular sticks of length 6 cm and 8 cm?

    (a) $48\,cm^2$ (b) $14\,cm^2$ (c) $24\,cm^2$ (d) $96\,cm^2$

4. Due to heavy storm an electric wire got bent as shown in the figure. It followed a mathematical shape. Answer the following questions below.

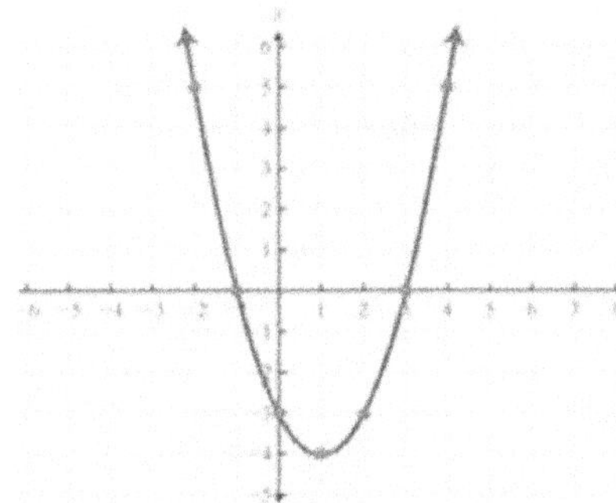

(i) Name the shape in which the wire is bent

    (a) spiral   (b) ellipse   (c) linear   (d) parabola

(ii) How many zeroes are there for the polynomial (shape of the wire)

    (a) 2   (b) 3   (c) 1   (d) 0

(iii) The zeroes of the polynomial are

    (a) $-1, 5$ (b) $-1, 3$ (c) $3, 5$ (d) $-4, 2$

(iv) What will be the expression of the polynomial?

    (a) x^2+2x-3 (b) x^2-2x+3 (c) x^2-2x-3 (d) x^2+2x+3

(v) What is the value of the polynomial if $x=-1$?

    (a) 6   (b) -18 (c) 18   (d) 0

Practice Case Study MCQs

5. A group of 5 students of class 10 went to an ice-cream parlor for the taste of ice-cream. Further, they decided to analyse the volume of ice-cream. In the figure, the ice-cream container is in the form of cone surmounted with ice-cream in hemispherical shape.

The radii of cone and hemispherical shape are equal to 3 cm and slant height of container is 5 cm.

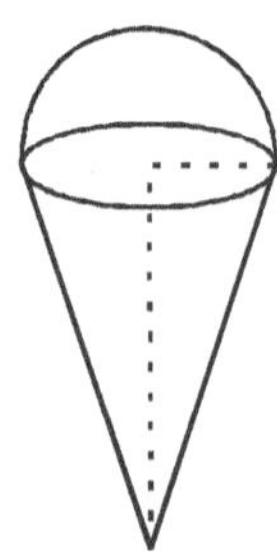

Answer the following questions.

(i) What is the formula to find the volume of hemisphere?

   (a) $\dfrac{4}{3}\pi r^2 h$ (b) $\dfrac{3}{4}\pi r^2 h$ (c) $\dfrac{2}{3}\pi r^3$ (d) $\dfrac{3}{2}\pi r^2 h$

(ii) What is the volume of ice-cream in hemispherical shape?

   (a) $18\pi\,cm^3$ (b) $24\pi\,cm^3$ (c) $27\pi\,cm^3$ (d) $20\pi\,cm^3$

(iii) What is the formula to find the volume of cone?

   (a) $\dfrac{2}{3}\pi r^2 h$ (b) $\dfrac{1}{3}\pi r^2 h$ (c) $\dfrac{4}{3}\pi r^2 h$ (d) $\dfrac{2}{3}\pi r h^2$

(iv) What is the volume of ice-cream in the container?

   (a) $12\pi\,cm^3$ (b) $16\pi\,cm^3$ (c) $20\pi\,cm^3$ (d) $24\,\pi\,cm^3$

(v) If the cost of filling ice-cream in the container is ₹7 per centimeter cube, then find the total cost of ice-cream in the container and surmounted part.

   (a) ₹ 640   (b) ₹ 660   (c) ₹ 670   (d) ₹ 760

6. The class X students are given a mathematical problem to discuss the properties of tangent to a circle and to evaluate some unknown angles of the figure shown below.

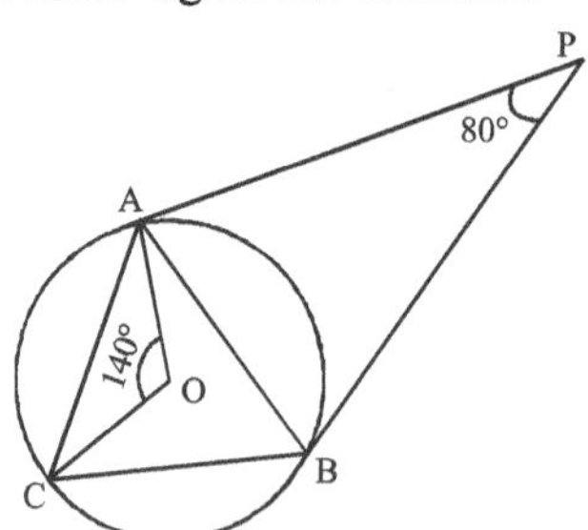

In the given figure O is the centre of the circum-circle of $\triangle ABC$. Tangents A and B intersect at P. If it is given that $\angle APB = 80°$ and $\angle AOC = 140°$.

Then answer the following questions.

(i) The number of possible tangents to a circle from a given point outside of the circle.

(a) 0   (b) 1   (c) 2   (d) infinite

(ii) Find $\angle PAB$

(a) $50°$ (b) $60°$ (c) $70°$ (d) $90°$

(iii) Find $\angle OAB$

(a) $30°$ (b) $40°$ (c) $50°$ (d) $60°$

(iv) Find $\angle OCA$

(a) $20°$ (b) $30°$ (c) $40°$ (d) $80°$

(v) Find $\angle CAB$

(a) $30°$ (b) $60°$ (c) $90°$ (d) $120°$

7. Students of class X were given a task to observe the application of arithmetic progression for the construction of staiyers at a football ground.

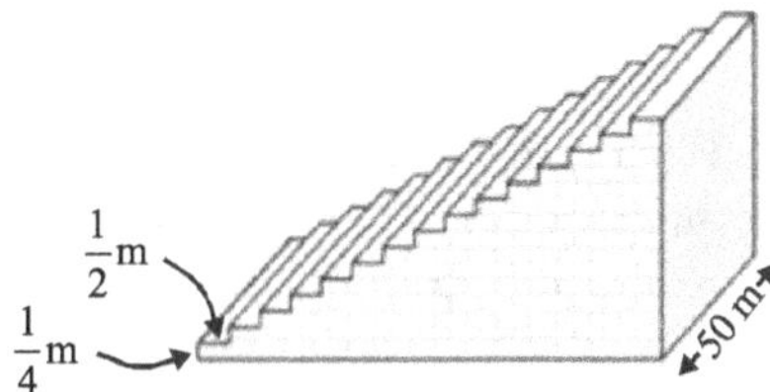

In the figure a small terrace at a football ground comprises of 15 steps each of which is 50 m long and built of solid concrete. Each step has a rise of $\frac{1}{4}$ m and a tread of $\frac{1}{2}$ m

Then, answer the following questions

(i) Volume of the concrete for the first step of terrace.

(a) $5\,m^3$ (b) $6.25\,m^3$ (c) $5.25\,m^3$ (d) $25\,m^3$

(ii) Volume of the concrete for the 8th step of terrace.

(a) $25\,m^3$ (b) $40\,m^3$ (c) $50\,m^3$ (d) $60\,m^3$

(iii) The common difference of A.P formed by the volume of steps of terrace.

(a) $\dfrac{25}{4}$ (b) $\dfrac{50}{4}$ (c) $\dfrac{58}{7}$ (d) $\dfrac{100}{4}$

(iv) Total volume of concrete required to build the terrace.

(a) $520\,m^3$ (b) $580\,m^3$ (c) $620\,m^3$ (d) $750\,m^3$

(v) If the rate of construction of terrace is ₹20 per metre cube, then total cost to build the terrace.

(a) ₹15000   (b) ₹20000   (c) ₹25000   (d) ₹35000

8. Two students Kabir and Rohan of class X were playing near the street lamp. At a time Kabir noticed the length of shadow of Rohan when he was running away from street lamp.

If the height of Rohan is 140 cm, the height street lamp is 4.6 m more than the height of Rohan and speed of Rohan is 4 m/s, then the length of Rohan's shadow is t after 8 s.

The figure of scenario is given below

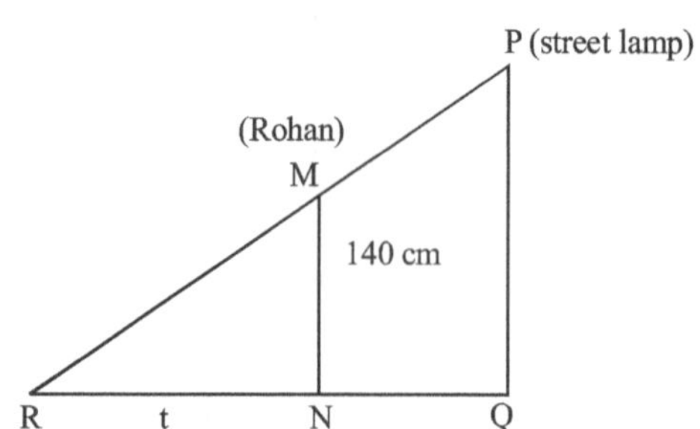

Now, answer the following questions.

(i) Which of the pair of triangles are similar?

   (a) $\Delta QPR \sim \Delta RMN$ (b) $\Delta PRQ \sim \Delta RNM$

   (c) $\Delta QRP \sim \Delta MNR$ (d) $\Delta PQR \sim \Delta MNR$

(ii) Distance of Rohan from street lamp after 8 seconds.

   (a) 22 m   (b) 27 m   (c) 32 m   (d) 38 m

(iii) Find the length of Rohan's shadow after 8s.

   (a) 9 m   (b) 9.73 m   (c) 12 m   (d) 13 m

(iv) The shortest distance between top of street lamp and the end of the shadow is

   (a) 42.15 m   (b) 41.73 m   (c) 50 m   (d) 40 m

(v) PQ is parallel to MN, then which of the following is true?

   (a) $\dfrac{MN+PQ}{PM+NQ} = \dfrac{MR}{NR}$ (b) $\dfrac{PR}{MR} = \dfrac{QR}{NR}$

   (c) $\dfrac{RM}{NQ} = \dfrac{PM}{RN}$ (d) $\dfrac{PR}{QN} = \dfrac{QR}{PM}$

9. Mukesh is having garden, their are some palm tree in garden. One day due to heavy rain and storm one of the trees got broken such that the top of the tree touches the ground, as shown in the figure.

The height of the unbroken part is 10 m and the distance between the foot of the tree to the point where the top touches the ground is $10\sqrt{3}\text{m}$.

Then answer the following questions.

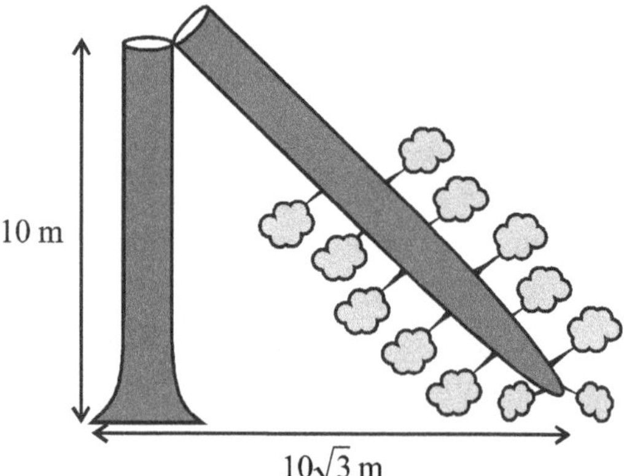

(i) What is length of the broken part?

(a) $20\sqrt{3}\,\text{m}$ (b) $20\,\text{m}$ (c) $\left(10+10\sqrt{3}\right)\text{m}$ (d) $30\,\text{m}$

(ii) What is the height of original tree?

(a) $20\,\text{m}$ (b) $30\,\text{m}$ (c) $\left(10+10\sqrt{3}\right)\text{m}$ (d) $10\,\text{m}$

(iii) The angle makes top of the tree with ground is:

(a) $45°$ (b) $60°$ (c) $30°$ (d) $90°$

(iv) What types of triangle can be formed?

(a) Right triangle (b) Scaleve triangle (c) Equilateral triangle (d) Isosceles triangle

(v) What is the perimeter of the formed triangle?

(a) $30\sqrt{3}\,\text{m}$ (b) $\left(30+10\sqrt{3}\right)\text{m}$ (c) $40\sqrt{3}\,\text{m}$ (d) $\left(20+10\sqrt{3}\right)\text{m}$

10. Rahul's mother wants to make Gulab Jamuns at home. She wants to make 30 Gulab Jamuns, each Gulab Jamun shaped like a cylinder with two hemispherical ends with length 6cm and diameter 2.8cm. Each Gulab Jamun required sugar syrup approximately 30% of its volume. Then answer the following questions.

(i) What is the length of cylindrical portion of Gulab Jamun?

(a) $3.2\,\text{m}$ (b) $4.2\,\text{m}$ (c) $4.8\,\text{m}$ (d) $6\,\text{m}$

(ii) The volume of each Gulab Jamun is :

(a) $30.23\,\text{cm}^3$ (b) $31.23\,\text{cm}^3$ (c) $28.30\,\text{cm}^3$ (d) $20.25\,\text{cm}^3$

(iii) The surface area of each Gulab Jamun is :

(a) $38.72\,\text{cm}^2$ (b) $38\,\text{cm}^2$ (c) $37.82\,\text{cm}^2$ (d) $87.32\,\text{cm}^2$

(iv) The volume of 30 Gulab Jamun is :

(a) $906.9\,\text{cm}^3$ (b) $936.9\,\text{cm}^3$ (c) $849\,\text{cm}^3$ (d) $607.5\,\text{cm}^3$

(v) The volume of sugar syrup required is :

(a) $272.07\,\text{cm}^3$ (b) $254.7\,\text{cm}^3$ (c) $281.07\,\text{cm}^3$ (d) $182.25\,\text{cm}^3$

11. Rakesh and Mohit playing a card game. Rakesh picked up a card from properly mixed cards numbered from 1 to 25.

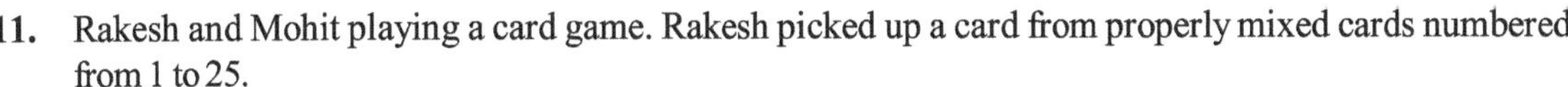

Then answer the following questions :

(i) The probability of getting prime numbers is :

(a) $\dfrac{9}{25}$ (b) $\dfrac{10}{25}$ (c) $\dfrac{7}{25}$ (d) $\dfrac{8}{25}$

(ii) The probability of getting multiple of 3 is :

(a) $\dfrac{7}{25}$ (b) $\dfrac{8}{25}$ (c) $\dfrac{6}{25}$ (d) $\dfrac{9}{25}$

(iii) The probability of getting multiple of 2 is :

(a) $\dfrac{10}{25}$ (b) $\dfrac{13}{25}$ (c) $\dfrac{12}{25}$ (d) $\dfrac{11}{25}$

(iv) The probability of getting multiple of 2 and 3 is :

(a) $\dfrac{3}{25}$ (b) $\dfrac{4}{25}$ (c) $\dfrac{2}{25}$ (d) $\dfrac{16}{25}$

(v) The probability of getting multiple of 2 or 3 is :

(a) $\dfrac{16}{25}$ (b) $\dfrac{4}{25}$ (c) $\dfrac{3}{25}$ (d) $\dfrac{10}{25}$

12. In a classroom, 4 friends are seated at the points P, Q, R and S as shown in Figure. Then answer the following questions.

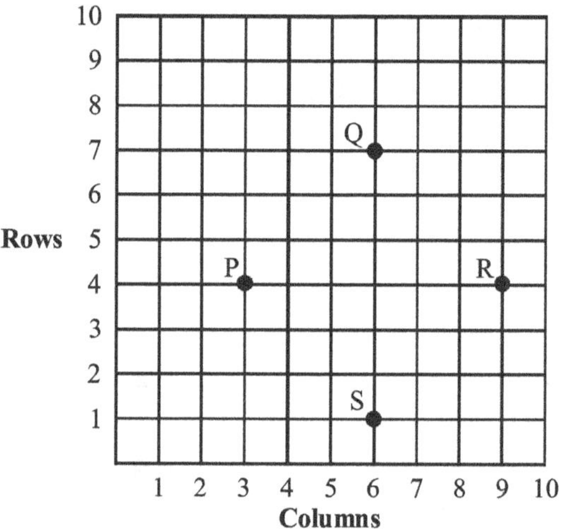

(i) The coordinate of P is :

(a) (4, 3)   (b) (3, 4)   (c) (6, 1)   (d) (6, 7)

(ii) The distance of PQ is :

(a) $3\sqrt{2}$ unit   (b) 4 unit   (c) $2\sqrt{3}$ unit   (d) 6 unit

(iii) The distance of PR is :

(a) 7 unit   (b) $6\sqrt{2}$ unit   (c) 6 unit   (d) 5 unit

(iv) The name of quadrilateral is :

(a) Square   (b) Rectangle   (c) Rhombus   (d) Parallelogram

(v) The mid point of QS is :

(a) (5, 4)   (b) (7, 4)   (c) (6, 2)   (d) (6, 4)

13. A girl of height 90 cm is walking away from the base of a lamp-post at a speed of 1.2 m/s. If the lamp is 3.6 m above the ground .

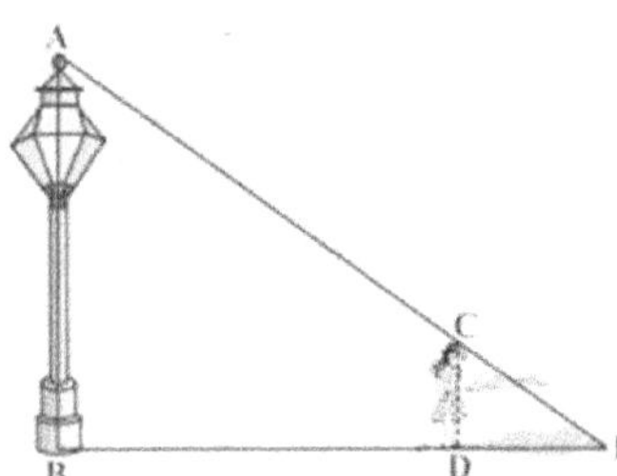

Answer the following questions.

(i) The length of her shadow after 4 seconds is :

    (a) 4.8m   (b) 1.6m   (c) 4m   (d) 2m

(ii) Distance travel by girl after 4 second is :

    (a) 4.8m   (b) 1.6m   (c) 4m   (d) 3m

(iii) Distance between their tops is :

    (a) 4m   (b) 1.8m   (c) 5.4m   (d) 3.2m

(iv) Similarity criterion of $\triangle ABE$ and $\triangle CDE$ is :

    (a) AA   (b) SSS   (c) SAS   (d) ASA

(v) Which of the following is true ?

    (a) $\angle B = \angle C$ (b) $\angle B = \angle D$ (c) $\angle A = \angle D$ (d) $\angle A = 90°$

14. To conduct sports day activities rectangular shaped school ground ABCD, lines have been drawn with chalk powder at a distance of 1m each. 100 flower pots have been placed at a distance of 1m from each other along AD, as shown in figure. Niharika, Nikita and Preet runs on 2nd, 5th and 8th line respectively.

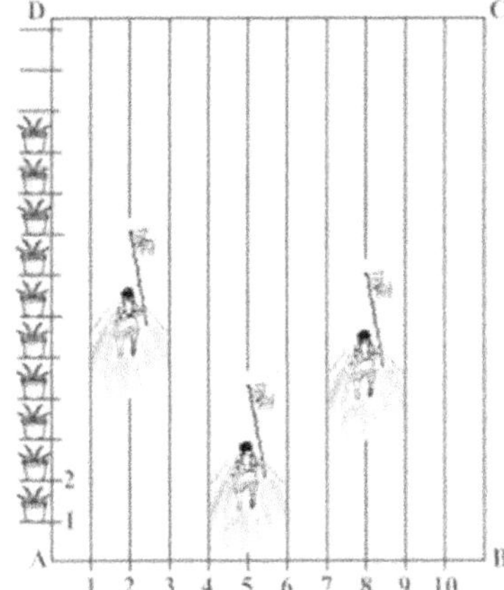

Answer the following questions.

(i) Niharika runs $\dfrac{1}{4}$ th the distance AD then her position is :

    (a) (20, 2)   (b) (2, 25)   (c) (20, 4)   (d) (25, 2)

(ii) If Nikita runs $\dfrac{1}{10}$ th the distance AD then her position is :

    (a) (5, 10)   (b) (10, 5)   (c) (20, 5)   (d) (10, 8)

(iii) If Preet runs $\dfrac{1}{5}$ th the distance AD then her position is :

    (a) (20, 8)   (b) (20, 5)   (c) (8, 20)   (d) (25, 8)

(iv) Distance between Niharika and Nikita is :

    (a) 15 unit   (b) 15.3 unit   (c) 16 unit   (d) 10 unit

(v) Distance between Nikita and Preet is :

    (a) 10.4 unit   (b) 14.4 unit   (c) 10 unit   (d) 14 unit

15. An electrician has to repair an electric fault on a pole of height 5m. He needs to reach a point 1.3 m below the top of the pole to under take the repair work. He place the ladder of length 7.4 m at that position.

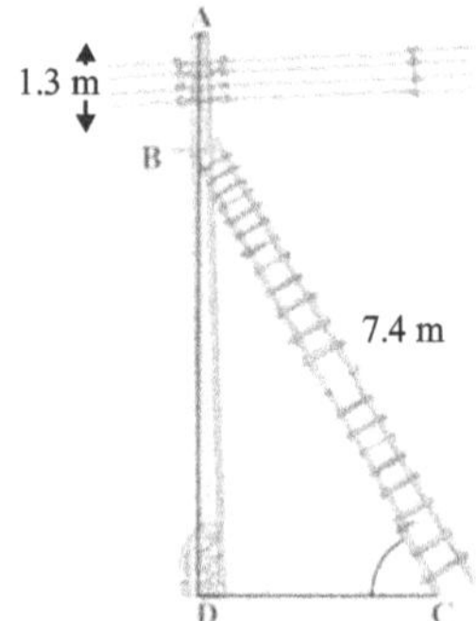

Then answer the following questions.

(i) Measure of $\angle C$ is :

    (a) 45°   (b) 60°   (c) 30°   (d) 90°

(ii) Measure of $\angle B$ is:

    (a) 60°   (b) 30°   (c) 45°   (d) 90°

(iii) Distance between foot of ladder and pole is:

    (a) 3.7 m   (b) $3.7\sqrt{3}$ m   (c) $3.7\sqrt{2}$ m   (d) $7.4\sqrt{3}$ m

(iv) The value of $\sin B$ is:

    (a) $\dfrac{1}{2}$ (b) 0   (c) 1   (d) $\dfrac{\sqrt{3}}{2}$

(v) The value of $\sin^2 B + \sin^2 C$ is

    (a) 1   (b) 0   (c) $\dfrac{1}{2}$ (d) $\dfrac{\sqrt{3}}{2}$

16. A horse is tied to a peg at one corner of a square shaped grass field of side 15m.   (Use $\pi = 3.14$)

Then answer the following questions.

(i) If rope of horse is 5m long then the area of that part of the field in which the horse can graze is :

(a) 19.625m²   (b) 29.625m²   (c) 19 m²   (d) 18.625m²

(ii) If rope of horse 10 m long then the area of that part of the field in which the horse can graze is:

(a) 68.5m²   (b) 78.5m²   (c) 58.5m²   (d) 73.5m²

(iii) The increase in the grazing area if the rope were 10m long instead of 5m.

(a) 58.875m²   (b) 58m²   (c) 57.875m²   (d) 68.87 m²

(iv) If rope of horse is 5 m long then the area of that part of the field in which the horse can not graze is:

(a) 204.37m²   (b) 200.37m²   (c) 205.37m²   (d) 205m²

(v) If rope of horse 10m long then the area of that part of the field in which the horse can not graze is :

(a) 146.5 m²   (b) 205.37m²   (c) 46.5m²   (d) 146 m²

17. The class X students of a secondary school in Krishinagar have been allotted a rectangular plot of land for their gardening activity. Sapling of Gulmohar are planted on the boundary at a distance of 1 m from each other. There is a triangular grassy lawn in the plot as shown in the figure. The students are to sow seeds of flowering plants on the remaining area of the plot.

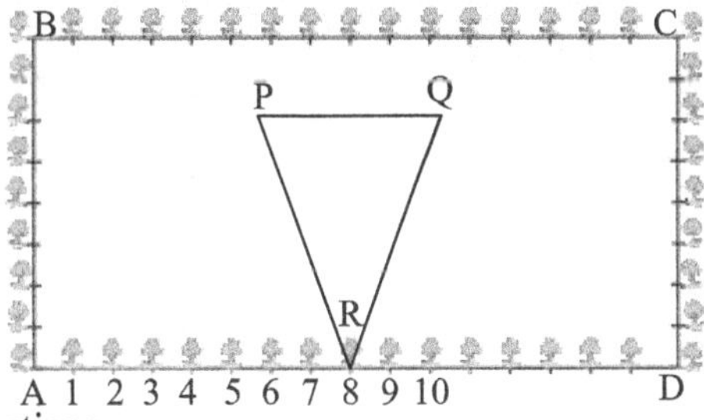

Answer the following questions.

(i) Taking A as the origin, the coordinate of R is:

(a) (8, 1)   (b) (8, 0)   (c) (0, 8)   (d) (1, 8)

(ii) Taking D as origin the coordinate of P is:

(a) (6, 6)   (b) (8, 6)   (c) (6, 10)   (d) (10, 6)

(iii) Taking A as the origin the coordinate of P is:

(a)   (10, 6)   (b)   (6, 6)   (c)   (6, 10)   (d)   (6, 0)

(iv) Taking A as the origin. Find distance between P and Q

(a)   6m   (b)   5m   (c)   4m   (d)   3m

(v) Find area of ΔPQR

(a) $12\,m^2$ (b) $10\,m^2$ (c) $14\,m^2$ (d) $8\,m^2$

18. Shakila put ₹ 500 into her daughter's money box when she was one year old, ₹ 550 on her second birthday, ₹ 600 on her third birthday and will continue in the same way.
Answer the following questions.

(i) How much money will be give on 18th birthday?
(a)   ₹ 1350   (b)   ₹ 1450
(c)   ₹ 2450   (d)   ₹ 1300

(ii) How much money will be give on n^{th} birthday?
(a)   ₹ $5(n+9)$ (b)   ₹ $50(n+9)$
(c)   ₹ $10(n+9)$ (d)   ₹ $50\,n$

(iii) How much money will be collected in the money box when daughter 20 years old?
(a)   ₹ 19500   (b)   ₹ 14000   (c)   ₹ 24500   (d)   ₹ 10500

(iv) How much money will be collected in the money box when daughter n years old?

(a)   ₹ $\dfrac{n}{2}(500+n)$ (b)   ₹ $\dfrac{n}{2}(1000+n)$ (c)   ₹ $\dfrac{5n}{2}(n+19)$ (d)   ₹ $\dfrac{50}{2}(n+19)$

(v) The common difference of A.P. is:
(a)   100   (b)   60   (c)   50   (d)   500

19. Students of class X make a design such that, the area of an equilateral triangle ABC is 17320.5 cm². With each vertex of the triangle as centre, a circle is drawn with radius equal to half the length of the side of the triangle. (Use $\pi = 3.14$ and $\sqrt{3} = 1.73205$)

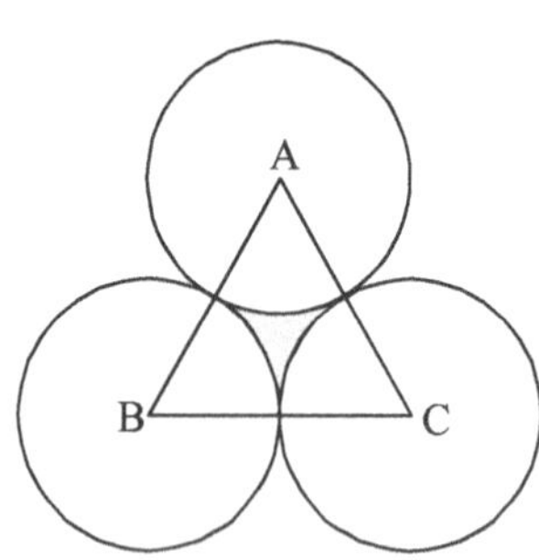

Answer the following questions.

(i) Find the length of side of $\triangle ABC$.

    (a) 200 cm   (b) 105.5 cm

    (c) 210.3 cm   (d) 200.5 cm

(ii) Find the radius circle.

    (a) 200 cm   (b) 20 cm

    (c) 10 cm   (d) 100 cm

(iii) Find the area of each sector.

    (a) $5233.3 \, cm^2$ (b) $5223.3 \, cm^2$ (c) $4233.3 \, cm^2$ (d) $522.2 \, cm^2$

(iv) Find the area of the shaded region.

    (a) $17320.5 \, cm^2$ (b) $1620.5 \, cm^2$ (c) $15700 \, cm^2$ (d) $31400 \, cm^2$

(v) Find the perimeter of $\triangle ABC$.

    (a) 60 cm   (b) 400 cm   (c) 600 cm   (d) 300 cm

20. A rectangular park is to be designed whose breadth is 4 m less than its length. Its area is to be 80 square metres more than the area of a park that has already been made in the shape of an isosceles triangle with its base as the breadth of the rectangular park and of altitude 12 m shown in figure.

Answer the following questions.

(i) Find the breadth of the park.

    (a) 8m   (b) 10m   (c) 80m   (d) 2m

(ii) Find the length of the park.

    (a) 8m   (b) 10m   (c) 14m   (d) 6m

(iii) Find the area of rectangular part of park.

    (a) $80 \, m^2$ (b) $140 \, m^2$ (c) $200 \, m^2$ (d) $60 \, m^2$

(iv) Find the area of triangular part of park.

    (a) $60 \, m^2$ (b) $140 \, m^2$ (c) $50 \, m^2$ (d) $80 \, m^2$

(v) Find the area of park.

    (a) $200 \, m^2$ (b) $140 \, m^2$ (c) $60 \, m^2$ (d) $160 \, m^2$

21. Class teacher of class X of school have been organised a drawing activity on a square handkerchief. One circular designs each of radius 7 cm are made shown in figure.

Answer the following questions.

(i) Find the length of side of square.

    (a) 21 cm   (b) 42 cm   (c) 14 cm   (d) 28 cm

(ii) Find the area of square.

    (a) $1764\,cm^2$ (b) $196\,cm^2$ (c) $49\,cm^2$ (d) $1760\,cm^2$

(iii) Find the diagonal of square.

    (a) $42\,cm$ (b) $28\,cm$ (c) $42\sqrt{2}\ cm$ (d) $42\sqrt{3}\ cm$

(iv) Find the area each circular design.

    (a) $49\,cm^2$ (b) $154\,cm^2$ (c) $196\,cm^2$ (d) $9\,cm^2$

(v) Find the area of the remaining portion.

    (a) $378\,cm^2$ (b) $564\,cm^2$ (c) $236\,cm^2$ (d) $64\,cm^2$

22. A timber merchant 200 logs are stacked in the following manner. 20 logs in the bottom row. 19 in the next row. 18 in the row next to it and so on shown in figure.

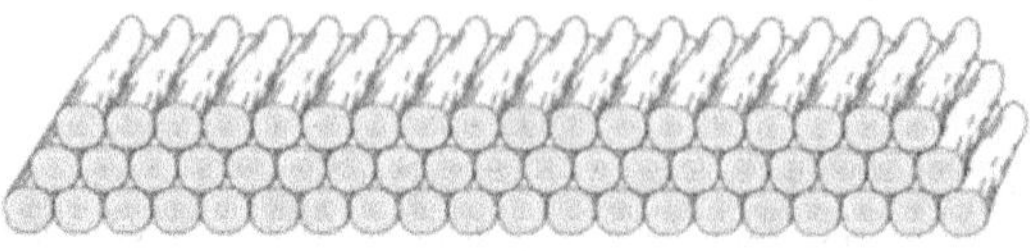

Answer the following questions.

(i) Find number of rows in which 200 logs are placed?

    (a)   5   (b)   25   (c)   16   (d)   10

(ii) How many logs are in the top row?

    (a)   16   (b)   25   (c)   5   (d)   9

(iii) How many logs are in the 5th row from bottom?

    (a)   16   (b)   5   (c)   25   (d)   9

(iv) How many logs are in the 5th row from top?

    (a)   16   (b)   5   (c)   20   (d)   9

(v) Difference between number of logs in top and bottom row.

    (a)   15   (b)   16   (c)   20   (d)   5

23. A telephone company wants to position a relay tower at P between A and B is such a way that the distance of the tower from B is twice its distance from A. If P lies on AB, shown in figure. If we take A as the origin 0, and 1 km as one unit on both the axis, the coordinates of B will be $(36, 15)$.

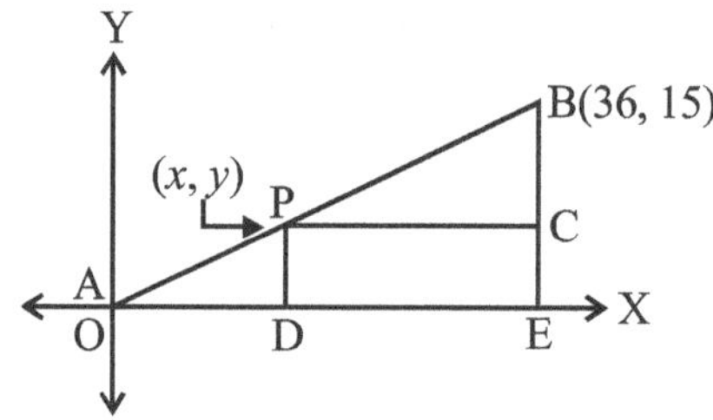

Answer the following questions.

(i) Find the ratio in which P divides AB.

    (a) $1:2$ (b) $2:1$ (c) $1:3$ (d) $3:1$

(ii) The coordinate of A is :

    (a) $(0,1)$ (b) $(1,0)$ (c) $(0,0)$ (d) $(1,1)$

(iii) The coordinate of P is :

    (a) $(16,5/2)$ (b) $(12,5)$ (c) $(5,12)$ (d) $(12,16)$

(iv) Find length AD.

    (a) 12 unit   (b) 5 unit   (c) 10 unit   (d) 7 unit

(v) Find length PB.

    (a) 10 unit   (b) 12 unit   (c) 25 unit   (d) 26 unit

24. Place a lighted bulb at a point O on the ceiling and directly below it a table in classroom. Place $\triangle ABC$ shape cardboard parallel to the ground between the lighted bulb and the table. Then a shadow of $\triangle A'B'C'$ is cost on the table such that $\triangle ABC \sim \triangle A'B'C'$ shown in figure.

If AB = 5 cm, A'B' = 15 cm; B'C' = 12 cm, AC = 3 cm, $\angle B' = 60°$ and $\angle A = 80°$.

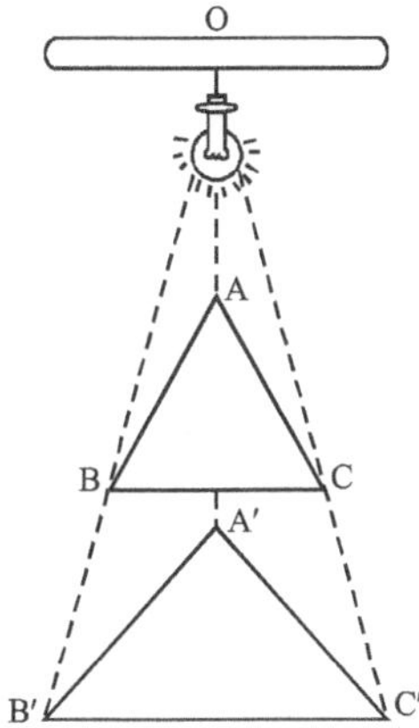

Answer the following questions.

(i) Length of A'C' is :

    (a) 3 cm   (b) 4 cm   (c) 9 cm   (d) 12 cm

(ii) Length of BC is :

    (a) 4 cm   (b) 12 cm   (c) 3 cm   (d) 15 cm

(iii) Measure of $\angle A'$ is :

    (a) $60°$ (b) $80°$ (c) $180°$ (d) $40°$

(iv) Find the measure of $\angle B$.

    (a) $60°$ (b) $40°$ (c) $80°$ (d) $180°$

(v) Find the measure of $\angle C$.

    (a) $60°$ (b) $40°$ (c) $80°$ (d) $180°$

25. Shanta runs an industry in a shed which is in the shape of a cuboid surmounted by a half cylinder shown in figure. If the base of the shed is of dimension 7 m × 15 m, and the height of the cuboidal portion is 8 m.

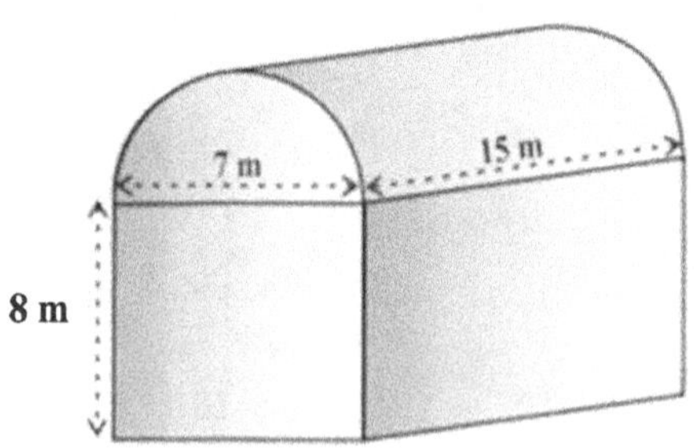

(Take $\pi = \dfrac{22}{7}$)

Answer the following questions.

(i) What is the surface area of shed?

  (a) $555\,m^2$ (b) $555.5\,m^2$ (c) $556.5\,m^2$ (d) $655.5\,m^2$

(ii) Find the cost of making shed at the rate of ₹50 per m^2.

  (a) ₹28750   (b) ₹70000   (c) ₹27775   (d) ₹27000

(iii) Find the volume of air that the shed can hold.

  (a) $1128.75\,m^3$ (b) $2318.75\,m^3$ (c) $3128.75\,m^3$ (d) $1128.75\,m^2$

(iv) If the machinery in the shed occupies a total space 300 m^3 then volume of air that the shed can hold is:

  (a) $828.75\,m^2$ (b) $828.75\,m^3$ (c) $820.75\,m^3$ (d) $808.75\,m^3$

(v) If the machinery in the shed occupies a total space 300 m^3 and there are 20 workers then volume of air per each workers is:

  (a) $41.4375\,m^3$ (b) $0.8\,m^3$ (c) $40.4\,m^3$ (d) $40.4375\,m^3$

26. Suppose a girl is sitting on the balcony of her house located on the bank of a river. She is looking down at a flower pot placed on a stair of a temple situated nearby on the other bank of the river. A right triangle is imagined to be made in this situation as shown in Figure. If the height of balcony is 20 m and angle between line of sight with horizontal in 30° then.

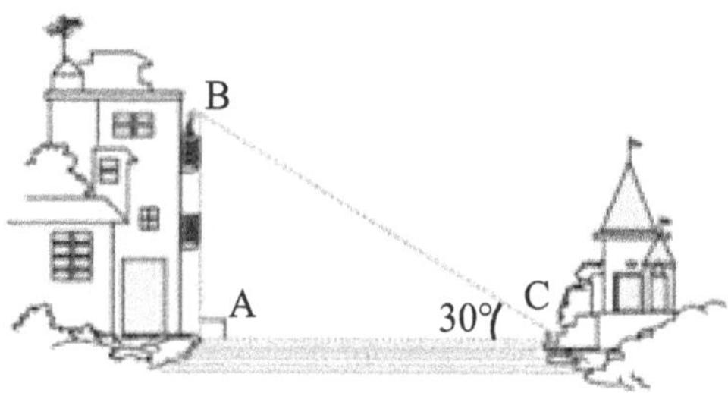

Answer the following questions.

(i) What is the width of the river?

  (a) $30\sqrt{2}\,m$ (b) $30\sqrt{3}\,m$ (c) $20\sqrt{3}\,m$ (d) $20\sqrt{2}\,m$

(ii) Length of line of sight BC is:

(a) $40\sqrt{3}$m   (b) 40m   (c) $30\sqrt{2}$m   (d) $30\sqrt{3}$m

(iii) What is the measure of $\angle B$?

(a) $60°$ (b) $30°$ (c) $45°$ (d) $90°$

(iv) The value of sin B – sinC is

(a) $\dfrac{1}{2}$ (b) $\dfrac{1}{\sqrt{3}}$ (c) $\dfrac{\sqrt{3}+1}{2}$ (d) $\dfrac{\sqrt{3}-1}{2}$

(v) The value of $\sec^2 B - \cot^2 C$ is

(a) 0 (b) 1 (c) $\dfrac{1}{2}$ (d) $\dfrac{4}{3}$

27. Nazima is fly fishing in a stream. The tip of her fishing rod is 1.8 m above the surface of the water and the fly at the end of the string rests on the water 3.6 m away and 2.4 m from a point directly under the tip of the rod. Assuming that her string (from the tip of her rod to the fly) is taut shown in figure.

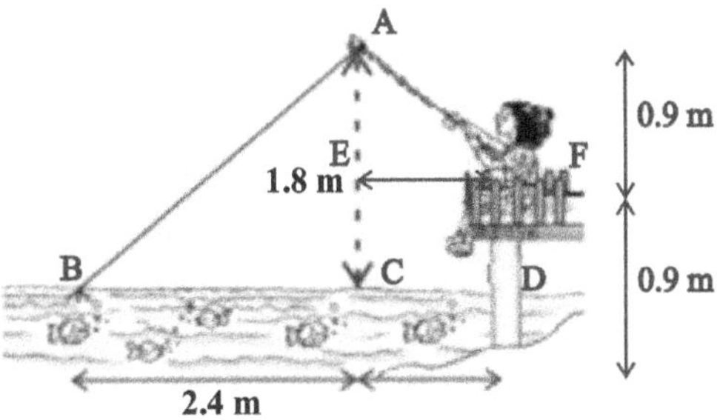

Answer the following questions.

(i) How much string does she have out?

(a) 1m   (b) 2m   (c) 3m   (d) 4m

(ii) Find the length of CD.

(a) 1m   (b) 1.2m   (c) 1.5m   (d) 2m

(iii) Find the length of her fishing rod.

(a) 1.5m   (b) 1.2m   (c) 1m   (d) 0.8m

(iv) Both triangles are similar by similarity criterion is:

(a) AAA   (b) SSS   (c) ASA   (d) SAS

(v) If she pulls in the string at the rate of 5 cm per second, then time taken to pulls all string.

(a) 1 min.   (b) 30 sec.   (c) 30 min.   (d) 40 sec.

28. In a potato race, a bucket is placed at the starting point, which is 3 m from the first potato, and the other potaotes are placed 2 m apart in a straight line. There are ten potatoes in the line shown in figure.

A competitor starts from the bucket, picks up the nearest potato, runs back with it, drops it in the bucket, runs back to pick up the next potato, runs to the bucket to drop it in, and she continues in the same way until all the potatoes are in the bucket.

Answer the following questions.

(i) Find the distance she has to run to pick up 1st potato.

    (a) 6m   (b) 8m   (c) 3m   (d) 16m

(ii) Find the distance she has to run to pick up 2nd potato.

    (a) 6m   (b) 8m   (c) 10m   (d) 5m

(iii) Find the distance she has to run to pick up 3rd potato.

    (a) 7m   (b) 14m   (c) 6m   (d) 10m

(iv) Find the common difference of AP.

    (a) 4m   (b) 1m   (c) 2m   (d) 3m

(v) What is the total distance the competitor has to run?

    (a) 200m   (b) 23m   (c) 240m   (d) 120m

29. Mohit and Deepa are studying in class-x and they are given an activity to design a board in the shape of triangle which circumscribe a circle.

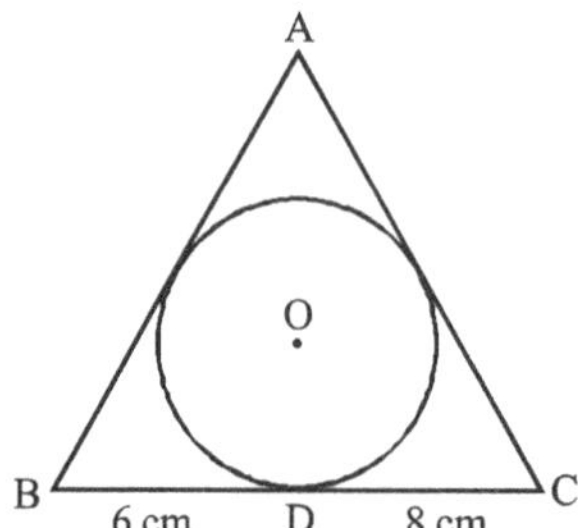

In the given design, a triangle $\triangle ABC$ is drawn to circumscribe a circle of radius 4 cm with centre O such that the segments BD and DC into which BC is divided by the point of contact D are of lengths 8 cm and 6 cm respectively. Then,

(i) area $(\triangle AB)$ is

    (a) 64 cm^2 (b) 70 cm^2 (c) 84 cm^2 (d) 92 cm^2

(ii) Length of AC

    (a) 12.68 cm   (b) 12 cm   (c) 14.28 cm   (d) 14 cm

(iii) Length of side AB

    (a) 8 cm   (b) 13 cm   (c) 15 cm   (d) 16 cm

(iv) Perimeter of $\triangle ABC$

    (a) 42 cm   (b) 48 cm   (c) 49 cm   (d) 52 cm

(v) Distance from the centre of circle to the vertex C of the triangle.

    (a) $4\sqrt{5}$ cm   (b) $5\sqrt{5}$ cm   (c) $6\sqrt{5}$ cm   (d) $5\sqrt{7}$ cm

30. Kartik and Aryan are the students of class-X. They are given a task to decorate the school's terrace. They put a ladder to go on the terrace whose length of rungs are decreasing. Then, few questions came to their mind regarding to the ladder.

In the figure, the ladder has rungs 25 cm apart. (see Fig.) The rungs decrease uniformly in length from 45 cm at the bottom to 25 cm at the top. If the top and the bottom rungs are $2\frac{1}{2}$ m apart.

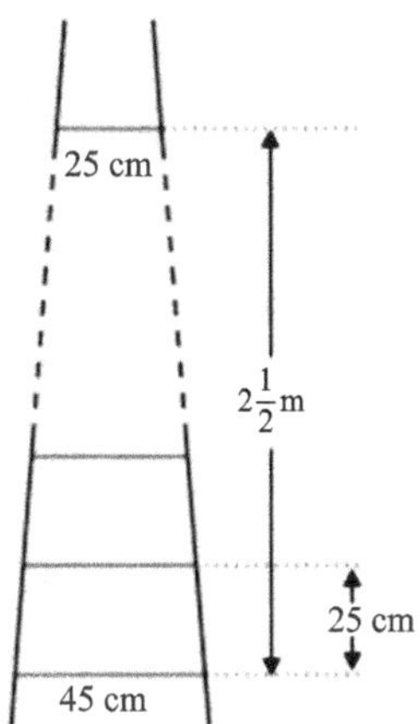

Then, answer the following questions.

(i) Number of rungs in the ladder.

    (a) 8   (b) 10   (c) 12   (d) 15

(ii) Length of rungs are uniformly decreasing by

    (a) 2.22 cm   (b) 3.22 cm   (c) 5.15 cm   (d) 2.65 cm

(iii) Length of 7th rung from bottom

    (a) 31.68 cm   (b) 40 cm   (c) $42\frac{1}{2}$ cm   (d) 43 cm

(iv) What is length of wood required for rungs?

    (a) 350 cm   (b) 400 cm   (c) 420 cm   (d) 430 cm

(v) Difference of length of 4th and 7th rungs.

    (a) 2.5 cm   (b) 3 cm   (d) 4 cm   (d) 6.66 cm

31. Ravi is studying in X standard. He is doing an activity to understand a solid figure shown in following figure. Few questions came to his mind while doing the activity. Give answers to his questions by looking at the figure in which diameter of cylindrical neck is $\left(\frac{2}{5}\right)^{th}$ of diameter of spherical part. (use $\pi = 3.14$)

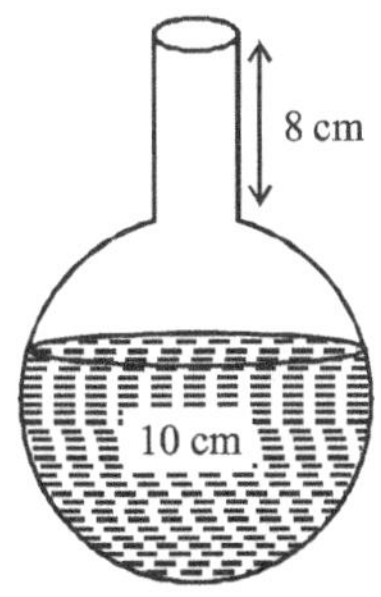

(i) Write the formula to find volume of spherical part.

(a) $\dfrac{2}{3}\pi r^3$　　(b) $\dfrac{4}{3}\pi r^2 h$　　(c) $\dfrac{4}{3}\pi r^3$　　(d) $\dfrac{1}{3}\pi r^2 h$

(ii) Find the radius of cylindrical neck.

(a) 1 cm　　(b) 1.5 cm　　(c) 2.0 cm　　(d) 0.5 cm

(iii) Find the volume (cm^3) of spherical part.

(a) 423.33　　(b) 523.33　　(c) 620.33　　(d) 650

(iv) Find the volume (cm^3) of cylindrical neck.

(a) 100.48　　(b) 85.28　　(c) 115.48　　(d) 107.08

(v) Find the total volume (cm^3) of solid figure.

(a) 618.23　　(b) 681.23　　(c) 632.18　　(d) 623.81

32. A group of class-X students went to see the national flag on the Red Fort which is on the wall of height 20 m.

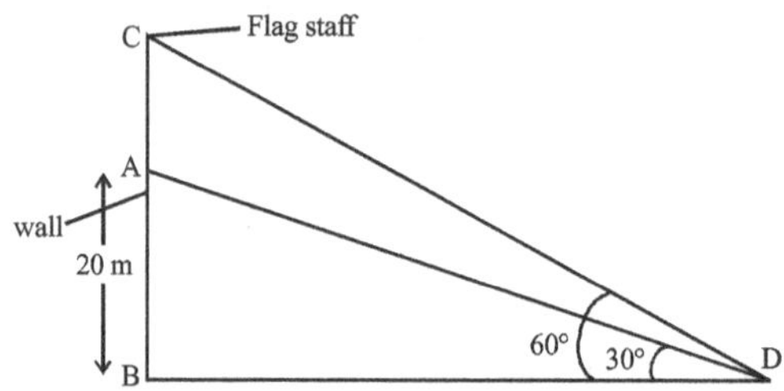

At a point on the ground, the angle of elevation of the foot and top of the flag are 30° and 60° as shown in the figure.

Few questions came to their mind while observing the flag.

(i) What is the length of BD?

(a) 34.64 m　　(b) 34 m　　(c) 43.64 m　　(d) 20 m

(ii) Find the length of flag.

(a) 20 m　　(b) 25 m　　(c) 40 m　　(d) 30 m

(iii) Find the difference of length of flag staff and wall.

(a) 20 m　　(b) 18.25 m　　(c) 10.5 m　　(d) 22.5 m

(iv) Find the value of 4 sin ∠ADB + 3 cos ∠BDC

(a) $\dfrac{7}{2}$　　(b) $\dfrac{1}{2}$　　(c) $\dfrac{5}{2}$　　(d) 2

(v) From the figure, find the length of AD.

(a) 10 m　　(b) 20 m　　(c) 30 m　　(d) 40 m

33. From a point P on the ground the angle of elevation of the top of a 10 m tall building is 30°. A flag is hoisted at the top of the building and the angle of elevation of the top of the flagstaff from P is 45°.

(take $\sqrt{3} = 1.732$)

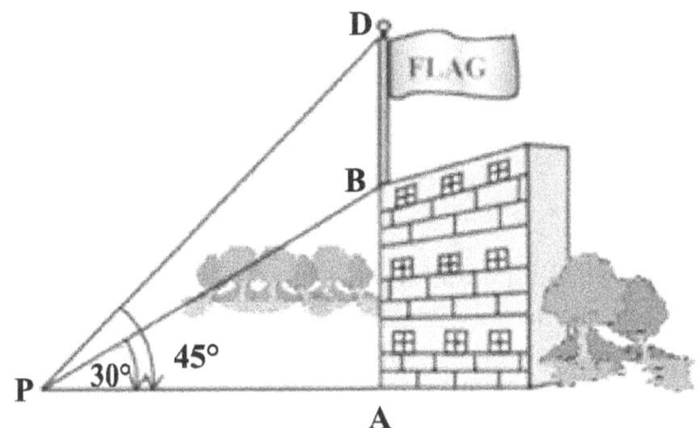

Answer the following questions.

(i) Find the distance of AP.
(a) 1.732 m   (b) 173.2 m   (c) 17.32 m   (d) 10 m

(ii) Find the length of PB.
(a) 20 m   (b) 10 m   (c) $20\sqrt{3}$ (d) $20\sqrt{3}$

(iii) Find the height of the flagstaff.
(a) 17.32 m   (b) 7.32 m   (c) 7 m   (d) 10 m

(iv) Find the length of PD.
(a) $10\sqrt{6}$ m   (b) 10 m   (c) $10\sqrt{3}$ m   (d) $10\sqrt{2}$ m

(v) Find the ratio of height of flagstaff and building.
(a) 82 : 5   (b) 3 : 5   (c) 183 : 250   (d) 181 :

34. A wooden article was made by scooping out a hemisphere from each end of a solid cylinder, as shown in Figure If the height of the cylinder is 10 cm. and its base is of radius 3.5 cm.

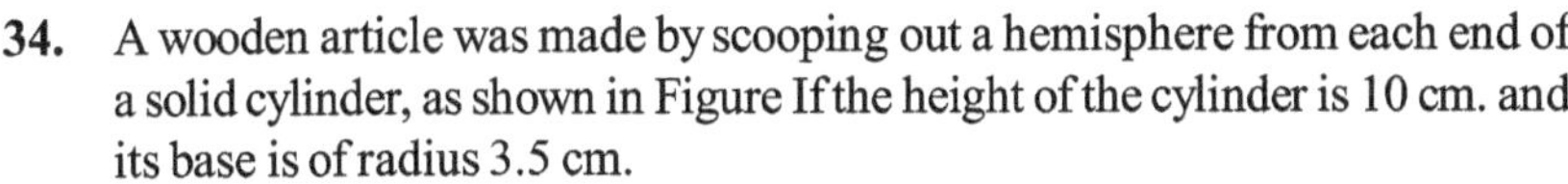

Answer the following questions.

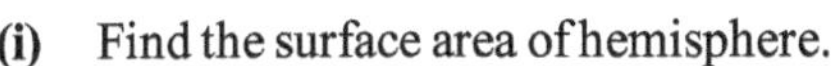

(i) Find the surface area of hemisphere.
(a) 76.5 cm^2 (b) 77 cm^2 (c) 77.5 cm^2 (d) 75.3 cm^2

(ii) Find the curved surface area of cylinder.
(a) 220 cm^2 (b) 220.5 cm^2 (c) 220.3 cm^2 (d) 110 cm^2

(iii) Find the total surface area of the article.
(a) 354 cm^2 (b) 374.34 cm^2 (c) 374 cm^2 (d) 375 cm^2

(iv) Find the volume of hemisphere.
(a) 89 cm^3 (b) 89.83 cm^3 (c) 90 cm^3 (d) 89.5 cm^3

(v) Find the volume of the article.
(a) 205.34 cm^3 (b) 205 cm^3 (c) 205.5 cm^3 (d) 200 cm^3

35. On school sport day, a sport teacher make a racing track whose left and right ends are semicircular shown in figure.

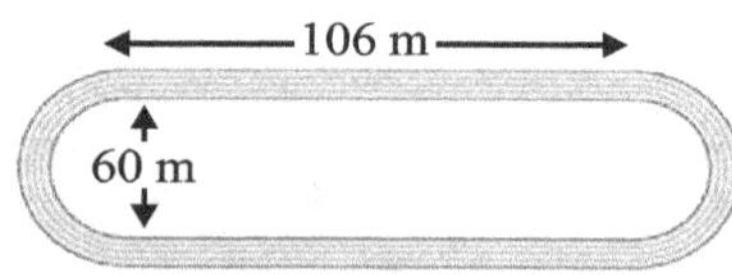

The distance between the two inner parallel line segments is 60 m and they are each 106 m long. If the track is 10 m wide then answer the following questions.

(i) Find the radius of inner semicircular end.

    (a)   30 m   (b)   60 m   (c)   10 m   (d)   40 m

(ii) Find the radius of outer semicircular end

    (a)   30 m   (b)   50 m   (c)   40 m   (d)   70 m

(iii) The distance around the track along its inner edge is :

    (a)   423.57 m   (b)   400.57 m   (c)   400.32 m   (d)   400 m

(iv) The distance around the track along its outer edge is :

    (a)   462.43 m   (b)   461.43 m   (c)   463 m   (d)   463.43 m

(v) Find the area of the track.

    (a)   4320 m^2 (b)   4230 m^2 (c)   2340 m^2 (d)   4120 m^2

36. Rahim is studying in class x. He is making a triangle in XY-cartesian plane shown in the figure, take O as origin.

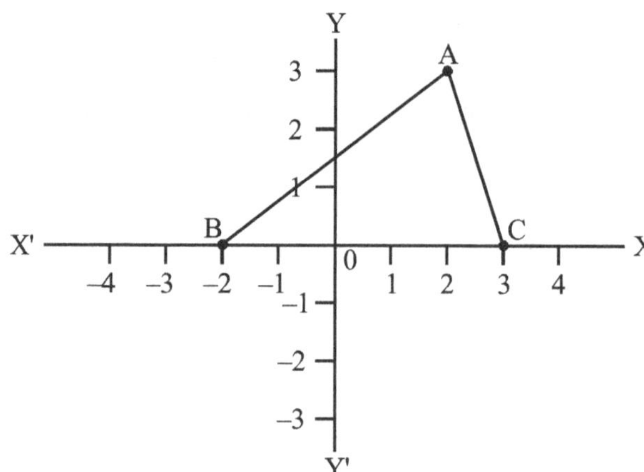

Answer the following questions.

(i) Write the coordinate of A.

    (a)   (3, 2)   (b)   (0, 3)   (c)   (2, 3)   (d)   (2, 0)

(ii) Write the coordinate of B.

(a) $(-2, 0)$ (b) $(2, 0)$ (c) $(3, 0)$ (d) $(0, -2)$

(iii) Find the distance between A and B.

(a) 4 unit   (b) $5\sqrt{2}$ unit   (c) 5 unit   (d) 6 unit

(iv) Write the coordidnate of C.

(a) $(0, 3)$ (b) $(3, 0)$ (c) $(-3, 0)$ (d) $(2, 0)$

(v) Find the mid-point of B and C.

(a) $\left(\dfrac{5}{2}, 0\right)$ (b) $(2, 0)$ (c) $(3, 0)$ (d) $\left(0, \dfrac{5}{2}\right)$

37. Radhika has seen a truck with a container fitted on its back carrying oil from one place to another. It is made of a cylinder with two hemispheres as its ends shown in figure. If diameter of cylinder is 3 m and length of container is 10 m.

Then answer the following questions.

(i) Find the height of cylinder.

(a) 10 m   (b) 3 m   (c) 7 m   (d) 1.9 m

(ii) Find the radius of hemisphere.

(a) 1.5 m   (b) 3 m   (c) 5 m   (d) 2.5 m

(iii) Find the surface area of container.

(a) $93.29 \, m^3$ (b) $94.29 \, m^2$ (c) $90.25 \, m^2$ (d) $91.25 \, m^2$

(iv) Find the volume of oil.

(a) $62.64 \, m^3$ (b) $61.64 \, m^3$ (c) $63.64 \, m^3$ (d) $60.64 \, m^3$

(v) If cost of each litre of oil is ₹ 50 then find the total cost.

(a) ₹ 3082   (b) ₹ 3152   (c) ₹ 3282   (d) ₹ 3182

38. A mathematics teacher of class X write three sequences on blackboard and based on sequences, she asked some questions with the students.

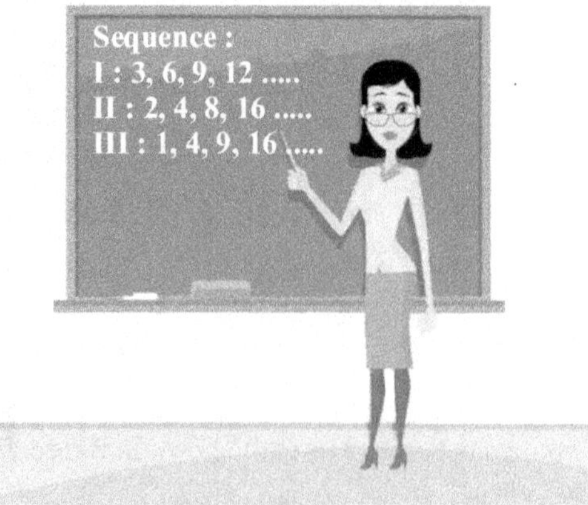

Then answer the following questions.

(i) Which of the given sequence is an arithmetic progression?

(a) I   (b) II   (c) III   (d) None of these

(ii) Write the formula of nth term of an AP.

(a) $a_n = a - (n-1)d$ (b) $a_n = a + (n-1)d$

(c) $a_n = a + (n-1)$ (d) $a_n = a(n-1)d$

(iii) Write the nth term of sequence I.

(a) $a_n = 3n$ (b) $a_n = 3(n+1)$ (c) $a_n = 3n + 2$ (d) $a_n = 3n + 1$

(iv) Write the 11th term of sequence I.

(a) 22   (b) 11   (c) 33   (d) 55

(v) Write the 7th term of sequence III.

(a) 25   (b) 49   (c) 36   (d) 100

39. A class teacher Dinesh of class X draw a figure on blackboard shown in figure. He asks following questions about figure.

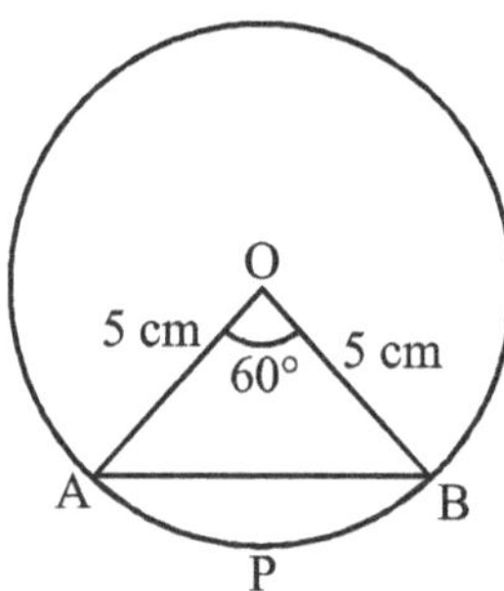

(i) Find the length of AB.

(a) 6 cm   (b) 7 cm   (c) 5 cm   (d) 10 cm

(ii) Find the area of circle.

(a) $77.5 \, \text{cm}^2$ (b) $78.57 \, \text{cm}^2$ (c) $72.0 \, \text{cm}^2$ (d) $73.23 \, \text{cm}^2$

(iii) Find the area minor sector

    (a) $13.09\,\text{cm}^2$ (b) $12.06\,\text{cm}^2$ (c) $11.09\,\text{cm}^2$ (d) $10.09\,\text{cm}^2$

(iv) Find the area of major sector

    (a) $65.48\,\text{cm}^2$ (b) $64.48\,\text{cm}^2$ (c) $63.48\,\text{cm}^2$ (d) $60.32\,\text{cm}^2$

(v) Find the length of arc APB

    (a) $6.25\,\text{cm}$ (b) $5.24\,\text{cm}$ (c) $7.5\,\text{cm}$ (d) $2.5\,\text{cm}$

40. Mathematics teacher of a class X organised an activity. He draw a line AB on XY plane shown in figure.

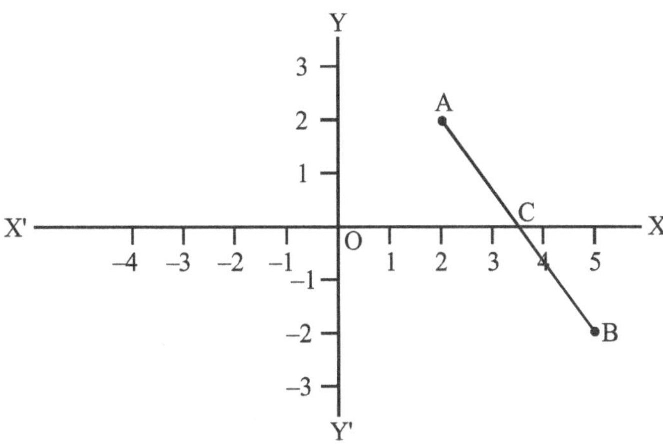

Answer the following questions.

(i) Find the coordinate of A.

    (a) $(-2, 2)$ (b) $(2, -2)$ (c) $(2, 2)$ (d) $(2, 3)$

(ii) Find the coordinate of B.

    (a) $(5, -2)$ (b) $(-2, 5)$ (c) $(2, 5)$ (d) $(5, 2)$

(iii) Find the distance of AB.

    (a) 6 unit   (b) 5 unit   (c) 9 unit   (d) 4 unit

(iv) Find the ratio in which X-axis divides the line segment AB.

    (a) $1:3$ (b) $2:1$ (c) $1:1$ (d) $1:2$

(v) Find the distance OB.

    (a) $\sqrt{29}$ unit   (b) $\sqrt{27}$ unit   (c) 5 unit   (d) 4 unit

41. Mahi and Shikha are students of class X. They are given a mathematical activity based on similar triangles. Mahi is trying to make similar triangle to shikha's triangle.

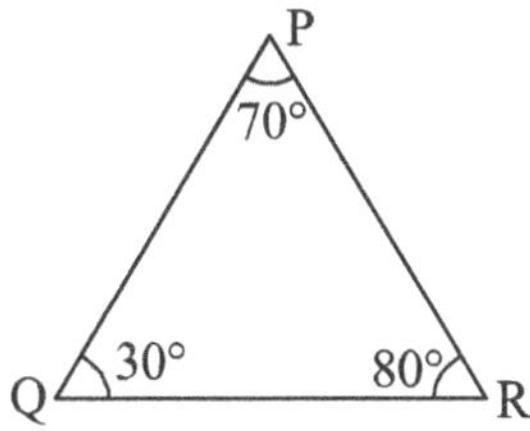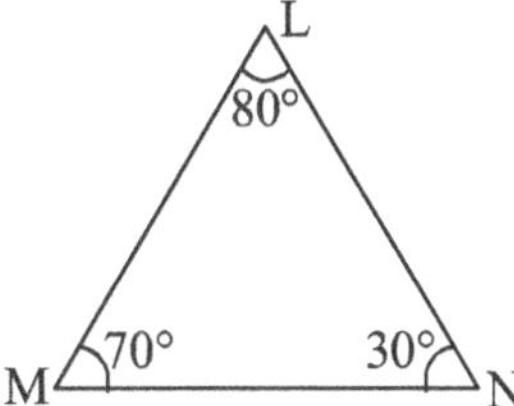

After drawing the triangles, class teacher asked the following questions to Mahi and Shika.

(i) By which similarity rule PQR and LMN are similar.

    (a) SSS   (b) ASA   (c) SAS   (d) AAA

(ii) Which of the similar order of $\triangle PQR$ and $\triangle LMN$

    (a) $\triangle PQR \sim \triangle LMN$ (b) $\triangle PQR \sim \triangle MNL$ (c) $\triangle PQR \sim \triangle NLM$ (d) $\triangle PQR \sim \triangle NML$

(iii) Which of the following is not a congruence rule?

    (a) SSS   (b) ASA   (c) AAA   (d) SAS

(iv) Compare the size of triangles.

    (a) Proportional   (b) Both equal

    (c) $\triangle PQR$ larger than $\triangle LMN$ (d) None of these

(v) Which side of $\triangle LMN$ correspond to side PQ of $\triangle PQR$.

    (a) LM   (b) MN   (c) LN   (d) None of these

42. Soniya and Anuj are students of class X and they given a polynomial such that "If one zero of the polynomial $3x^2 - 8x + 2k + 5$ is four times the other $4x^2 - 12x + 3k + 8$.

Then, answer the following questions.

(i) Find the sum of zeroes.

    (a) 3   (b) 4   (c) $\dfrac{12}{3}$ (d) $\dfrac{12}{5}$

(ii) For quadratic polynomial $ax^2 + bx + c$, $a \neq 0$, write the formula to find product of zeroes.

    (a) $\dfrac{b}{a}$ (b) $-\dfrac{b}{a}$ (c) $-\dfrac{c}{a}$ (d) $\dfrac{c}{a}$

(iii) If α and β be the zeroes of given polynomial. Then, what is the relation between α and β?

    (a) $\alpha + \beta = 4$ (b) $\alpha\beta = 4$ (c) $\beta = 4\alpha$ (d) $\alpha^2 = 16\beta$

(iv) If α and β be the zeroes of the given polynomial, then find value of α.

    (a) $\dfrac{1}{5}$ (b) $\dfrac{7}{4}$ (c) $\dfrac{2}{5}$ (d) $\dfrac{3}{5}$

(v) Find the value of k. If α and β be the zeroes of given polynomials.

    (a) $\dfrac{56}{75}$ (b) $-\dfrac{56}{75}$ (c) $\dfrac{75}{56}$ (d) $\dfrac{65}{75}$

43. Each student of class X were offered pizza in school's annual function. Next day in the school, each student were asked several questions of the given figure.

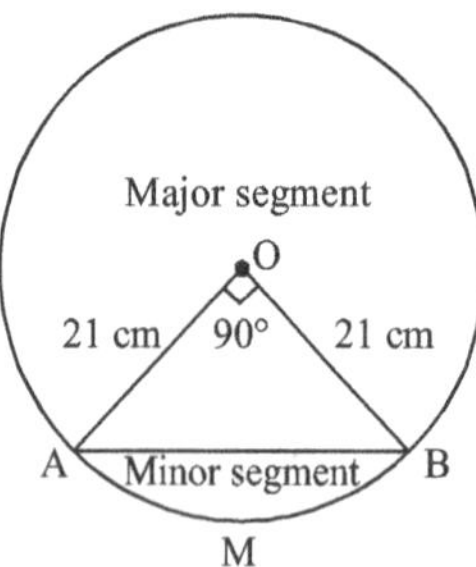

(i) Write the formula to find the area of circle.

(a) $\dfrac{\pi r^2}{2}$ (b) $2\pi r^2$ (c) $\dfrac{\pi r^2}{2+r}$ (d) πr^2

(ii) Write the formula to find the area of a sector of a circle.

(a) $\pi r^2 \dfrac{\theta}{360°}$ (b) $\dfrac{\theta}{360°} \times 2\pi r$ (c) $\dfrac{\theta}{180°} \times \pi r^2$ (d) $\dfrac{\theta}{360°} \times \pi r$

(iii) Find the area of major sector.
(a) 1039.5 cm^2 (b) 1025.5 cm^2 (c) 1051.5 cm^2 (d) 1550.5 cm^2

(iv) Find the area of minor segment.
(a) 122 cm^2 (b) 146 cm^2 (c) 126 cm^2 (d) 152 cm^2

(v) Find the area of major segment.
(a) 1602 cm^2 (b) 1260 cm^2 (c) 1620 cm^2 (d) 1026 cm^2

44. Ankit and Ranjan are given a task to stick posters on school's main gate at the height of 6 m. They need to reach a point 1.5 m below the top of they gate as shown in the figure.

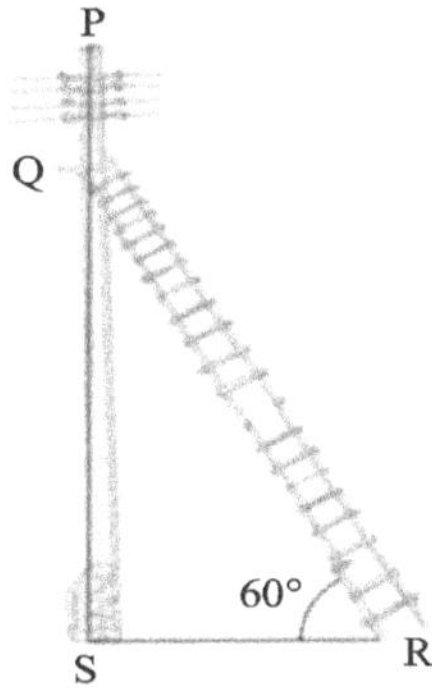

After completing the task they were asked following questions.

(i) Find the length of QS.
(a) 5.4m (b) 4.5m (c) 3.2m (d) 4.2m

(ii) Find the length of SR.
(a) 3.8m (b) 1.5m (c) 2.6m (d) 1.9m

(iii) Find the length of the ladder.
(a) 5.19m (b) 5.32m (c) 4.19m (d) 4.64m

(iv) If angle between ladder and horizontal is 45°, then which of the following is correct?
(a) QS = SR (b) QS = QR (c) PS = QR (d) SR + PQ = QS

(v) The line of sight is the line that drawn from the
(a) eye of an observer to the point in the object viewed by the observer
(b) the horizontal line
(c) vertical line
(d) None of the above

Case Study Based MCQs Solution

1. (i) (b) Cloth material required $= 2 \times$ S A of hemispherical dome

$$= 2 \times 2\pi\, r^2$$

$$= 2 \times 2 \times \frac{22}{7} \times (2.5)^2\, m^2$$

$$= 78.57\, m^2$$

  (ii) (a) Volume of a cylindrical pillar $= \pi\, r^2 h$

  (iii) (b) Lateral surface area $= 2 \times 2\pi r h$

$$= 4 \times \frac{22}{7} \times 1.4 \times 7\, m^2$$

$$= 123.2\, m^2$$

  (iv) (d) Volume of hemisphere $= \dfrac{2}{3}\pi\, r^3$

$$= \frac{2}{3}\ \frac{22}{7}\ (3.5)^3\, m^3$$

$$= 89.83\, m^3$$

  (v) (b) Sum of the volumes of two hemispheres of radius 1 cm each

$$= 2 \times \frac{2}{3}\,\pi 1^3$$

Volume of sphere of radius 2 cm

$$= \frac{4}{3}\,\pi 2^3$$

So, required ratio is $\dfrac{2 \times \dfrac{2}{3}\pi 1^3}{\dfrac{4}{3}\pi 2^3} = 1:8$

2. (i)   (c) (0,0)
  (ii) (a) (4,6)
  (iii) (a) (6,5)
  (iv) (a) (16,0)
  (v)   (b) (−12,6)

3. (i)   (c) 90°
  (ii) (b) SAS
  (iii) (b) 4 : 9

      (iv) (d) Converse of Pythagoras theorem

      (v) (a) $48\,\text{cm}^2$

4. (i) (d) parabola

      (ii) (a) 2

      (iii) (b) $-1, 3$

      (iv) (c) $x^2 - 2x - 3$

      (v) (d) 0

5. (i) (c) Volume of hemisphere $= \dfrac{2}{3}\pi r^3$

      (ii) (a) $\because$ Radius of hemispherical shape is 3 cm.

           $\therefore$ Volume of ice-cream in hemispherical shape is

$$= \frac{2}{3}\pi r^3 \;=\; \frac{2}{3}\pi(3)^3 \;=\; 18\pi\,\text{cm}^3$$

      (iii) (b) Volume of cone $= \dfrac{1}{3}\pi r^2 h$

      (iv) (a) $\because$ Slant height $(l) = 5$ cm

           $\therefore$ Height (h) of the container

$$= \sqrt{l^2 - r^2} = \sqrt{25 - 9}$$
$$= \sqrt{16} = 4$$

           $\therefore$ Volume of ice-cream in the container

$$= \frac{1}{3}\pi r^2 h \;=\; \frac{1}{3}\pi \times (3)^2 \times (4)$$
$$= 12\pi\,\text{cm}^3$$

      (v) (b) Total volume of ice-cream

           = Volume of ice-cream in the container + Volume of ice-cream in spherical shape.

$$= 18\pi + 12\pi = 30\pi\,\text{cm}^3$$

           Rate of filling ice-cream $= ₹7$ per cm^3

$$\therefore \text{ Total cost of ice-cream} = ₹7 \times 30 \times \frac{22}{7}$$
$$= ₹660$$

6. (i) (c) 2

      (ii) (a) Since, PA and PB are tangent to the circle from the external point P.

           $\therefore$ PA = PB

           In $\triangle$APB,

           PA = PB

$\Rightarrow \angle\, PAB = \angle\, PBA$ [angles opposite to equal sides of a triangle are equal]

By angle sum property in $\triangle APB$

$\angle\, PAB + \angle\, PBA + \angle\, APB = 180°$

$\angle\, PAB + \angle\, PBA + 80 = 180°$ $[\because \angle\, PBA = \angle\, PAB]$

$2\angle\, PAB = 180 - 80 = 100°$

$$\angle PAB = \frac{100°}{2} = 50°$$

(iii) (b) Since, tangents are perpendicular to radius of the circle

$\therefore OA \perp AP$

$\therefore \ \angle\, OAP = 90°$

Then, $\angle\, OAB = \angle\, OAP - \angle\, PAB$

$= 90° - 50° = 40°$ $(\because \ \angle\, PAB = 50°)$

(iv) (a) In $\triangle OAC$

$OA = OC$

$\Rightarrow \angle\, OAC = \angle\, OCA$ $[\because$ angle opposite to equal sides are equal]

By angle sum property in $\triangle OAC$

$\angle\, OAC + \angle\, OCA + \angle\, AOC = 180°$

$\angle\, OAC + \angle\, OCA + 140 = 180°$

$2\angle\, OCA = 180° - 140° = 40$

$\angle\, OCA = 20°$

(v) (b) $\angle\, OAC = \angle\, OCA = 20°$

$\therefore \ \angle\, CAB = \angle\, OAC + \angle\, OAB$

$= 20° + 40° = 60°$

7. (i) (b) Volume of concrete required for the first step of terrace $= \dfrac{1}{4} \times \dfrac{1}{2} \times 50 = 6.25 \text{ m}^3$

(ii) (c) Volume of concrete required for the 8th step of terrace $= 8 \times \dfrac{1}{4} \times \dfrac{1}{2} \times 50 = 50 \text{ m}^3$

(iii) (a) The A.P. formed by the volume of concrete required to build the first step, second step, third step,.........,fifteenth step

$$= \frac{1}{4} \times \frac{1}{2} \times 50, \left(2 \times \frac{1}{4}\right) \times \frac{1}{2} \times 50, \left(3 \times \frac{1}{4}\right)$$

$$\times \frac{1}{2} \times 50, \ldots, \left(15 \times \frac{1}{4}\right) \times \frac{1}{2} \times 50$$

$$= \frac{50}{8}, 2 \times \frac{50}{8}, 3 \times \frac{50}{8}, \ldots, 15 \times \frac{50}{8}$$

$\therefore$ The common difference of A.P. formed by volume of steps of terrace

$$= 2 \times \frac{50}{8} - \frac{50}{8} = \frac{50}{8} = \frac{25}{4}$$

(iv) (d) Total volume of concrete required to build the terrace

$$= 1 \times \frac{50}{8} + 2 \times \frac{50}{8} + 3 \times \frac{50}{8} + \dots\dots + 15 \times \frac{50}{8}$$

$$= \frac{50}{8}[1 + 2 + 3 + \dots + 15]$$

$$= \frac{50}{8} \times \frac{15}{2}[2 \times 1 + (15 - 1) \times 1]$$

$$= \frac{50}{8} \times \frac{15}{2} \times 16 = 750 \text{ m}^3$$

(v) (a) Total cost to build the terrace

$= ₹20 \times$ Total volume of concrete

$= ₹20 \times 750 = ₹15000$

8. (i) (d) In ΔPQR and ΔMNR,

$\angle Q = \angle N = 90°$

$\angle R = \angle R$ [common angle]

$\therefore$ By AA-similarity criterion

$\Delta PQR \sim \Delta MNR$

(ii) (c) Distance of Rohan form the pole of street lamp (QN) = speed $\times$ time

$= 4 \times 8 = 32 \text{ m}.$

(iii) (b) $\because \Delta PQR \sim \Delta MNR,$

$$\frac{QR}{RN} = \frac{PQ}{MN} \Rightarrow \frac{QN + RN}{RN} = \frac{4.6 + 1.4}{1.4}$$

$$\Rightarrow \frac{32 + t}{t} = \frac{6.0}{1.4}$$

$$\Rightarrow 32 \times 1.4 + 1.4t = 6t$$

$$\Rightarrow 6t - 1.4t = 44.8$$

$$\Rightarrow 4.6t = 44.8 \Rightarrow t = \frac{44.8}{4.6} = 9.73 \text{ m}$$

(iv) (a) $\because PQ = 6m, RQ = t + QN = 9.73 + 32$

$= 41.73$

By Pythagoras theorem in right $\Delta PQR,$

$$PR = \sqrt{PQ^2 + QR^2}$$

$$= \sqrt{36 + 1741.39} = 42.15 \text{ m}$$

(v) (b) Since, MN divides PR and QR and MN $\parallel$ PQ

$\Rightarrow$ MN divides PR and QR in the same ratio

$$\Rightarrow \frac{PM}{MR} = \frac{QN}{NR} \Rightarrow \frac{PM}{MR} + 1 = \frac{QN}{NR} + 1$$

$$\Rightarrow \frac{PM+MR}{MR} = \frac{QN+NR}{NR} \Rightarrow \frac{PR}{MR} = \frac{QR}{NR}$$

9. (i) (b) $AC = \sqrt{AB^2 + BC^2}$

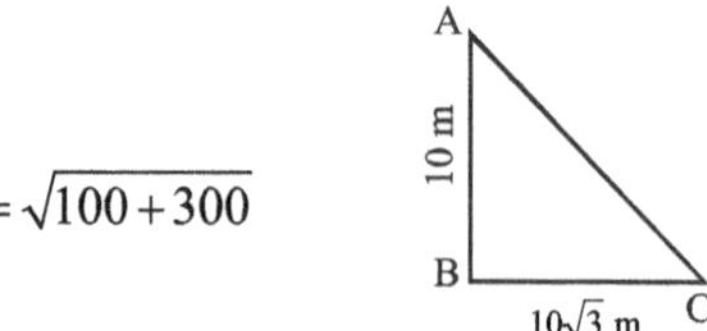

$$= \sqrt{100 + 300}$$

$$= 20 \, m$$

$\therefore$ Length of the broken part $= 20$ m

(ii) (b) Height of original tree $= 10 + 20 = 30$ m

(iii) (c) $\tan C = \dfrac{P}{B} = \dfrac{AB}{BC} = \dfrac{10}{10\sqrt{3}}$

$$\tan C = \frac{1}{\sqrt{3}} \Rightarrow \angle C = 30°$$

(iv) (a) $\because \angle B = 90°$

$\therefore$ $\triangle ABC$ is right triangle

(v) (b) Perimeter of $\triangle ABC = 10 + 20 + 10\sqrt{3}$

$$= (30 + 10\sqrt{3}) \, m$$

10. (i) (a) Length of cylindrical portion
$$= 6 - 2.8 = 3.2 \, m$$

(ii) (b) Volume of one Gulab Jamun

$= $ Volume of cylinder $+ 2 \times$ vol. hemisphere

$$= \pi r^2 h + 2 \times \frac{2}{3} \pi r^3$$

$$= \pi r^2 \left(h + \frac{4}{3} r \right)$$

$$= \frac{22}{7} \times (1.4)^2 \left(3.2 + \frac{4}{3} \times 1.4 \right)$$

$$= \frac{22}{7} \times \overset{0.2}{\cancel{1.4}} \times 1.4(3.2 + 1.87)$$

$$= 31.23 \text{ cm}^3$$

  (iii) (a) Surface area of one Gulab Jamun

$$= \text{C.S.A of cylinder} + 2 \times \text{C.S.A of hemisphere}$$
$$= \pi r h + 2 \times 2\pi r^2 = \pi r \,(h + 4r)$$

$$= \frac{22}{7} \times \overset{0.2}{\cancel{1.4}}\,(3.2 + 5.6) = 38.72 \text{ cm}^2$$

  (iv) (b) Volume of 30 Gulab Jamuns
$$= 30 \times 31.23 = 936.9 \text{ cm}^3$$

  (v) (c) Volume of sugar syrup $= 936.9 \times \dfrac{30}{100}\, 281.07 \text{ cm}^3$

11. (i) (a) Total card $= 25$

        No. of prime numbers $= 9$

$$\therefore \quad P(\text{prime numbers}) = \frac{9}{25}$$

  (ii) (b) No. of multiple 3 cards $= 8$

$$\therefore \quad P(\text{multiple of 3}) = \frac{8}{25}$$

  (iii) (c) No. of multiple of 2 cards $= 12$

$$\therefore \quad P(\text{multiple of 2}) = \frac{12}{25}$$

  (iv) (b) No. of multiple of 2 and 3 cards   (i.e multiple of 6) $= 4$

$$\therefore \quad P(\text{multiple of 2 and 3}) = \frac{4}{25}$$

  (v) (a) No. of multiple of 2 or 3
$$= 8 + 12 - 4 = 16$$

$$\therefore \quad P(\text{multiple of 2 or 3}) = \frac{16}{25}$$

12. (i) (b) Coordinate of P $= (3, 4)$

  (ii) (a) P(3, 4) & Q(6, 7)

$$PQ = \sqrt{(6-3)^2 + (7-4)^2} = \sqrt{9+9}$$

$$= 3\sqrt{2} \text{ unit}$$

(iii) (c)   P(3, 4) & R(9, 4)

$$PR = \sqrt{(9-3)^2 + (4-4)^2} = \sqrt{6^2 + 0}$$

$$= 6 \text{ unit}$$

(iv) (a)   P(3, 4), Q(6, 7), R(9, 4) and S(6, 1)

$$QR = \sqrt{(9-6)^2 + (4-7)^2}$$

$$= \sqrt{9+9} = 3\sqrt{2} \text{ unit}$$

$$RS = \sqrt{(9-6)^2 + (4-1)^2}$$

$$= \sqrt{9+9} = 3\sqrt{2} \text{ unit}$$

$$PS = \sqrt{(6-3)^2 + (1-4)^2}$$

$$= \sqrt{9+9} = 3\sqrt{2} \text{ unit}$$

$$PQ = 3\sqrt{2} \text{ unit}$$

∴   PQ = QR = RS = PS
All sides equal
PR = 6 unit

$$QS = \sqrt{(6-6)^2 + (7-1)^2} = 6 \text{ unit}$$

∴   PR = QR
Diagonals is also equal
So, ABCD is square.

(v) (d)   Mid-point of $QS = \left(\dfrac{6+6}{2}, \dfrac{7+1}{2} \right)$

$$= (6, 4)$$

13. ∵ ∠B = ∠D = 90°

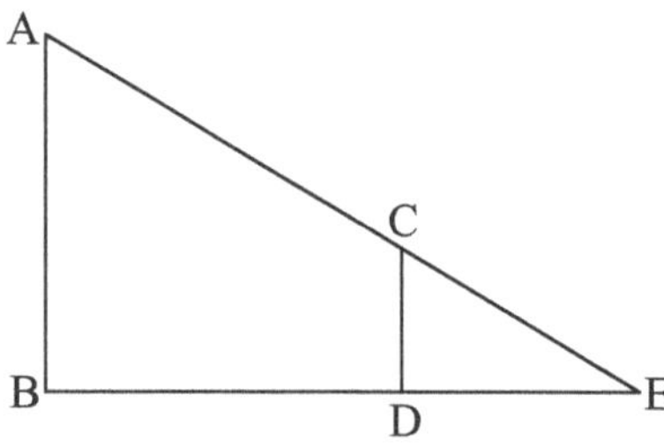

∠E = ∠E (common)
By AA = Similarity

$\triangle ABE \sim \triangle CDE$

$$\therefore \frac{AB}{CD} = \frac{BE}{DE} = \frac{AE}{CE} \qquad \ldots (1)$$

(i)   (b)   Distance $BD = S \times T = 1.2 \times 4 = 4.8$ m from (1)

$$\frac{AB}{CD} = \frac{BE}{DE} \Rightarrow \frac{3.6}{0.9} = \frac{4.8 + DE}{DE}$$

$$4 = \frac{4.8 + DE}{DE} \Rightarrow DE = 1.6m$$

(ii)   (a)

(iii)   (c) $CE = \sqrt{(1.6)^2 + (0.9)^2} = 1.8m$

$$\frac{AB}{CD} = \frac{AE}{CE} \Rightarrow \frac{3.6}{0.9} = \frac{AC + 1.8}{1.8}$$

$$\Rightarrow 4 = \frac{AC + 1.8}{1.8} \Rightarrow AC = 5.4m$$

(iv)   (a)

(v)   (b)

14.   (i)   (b)

     (ii)   (a)

     (iii)   (c)

     (iv)   (b)   Distance

$$= \sqrt{(25 - 10)^2 + (2 - 5)^2} = \sqrt{15^2 + 3^2}$$

$$= \sqrt{234} = 15.3 \, \text{unit}$$

     (v)   (a)   Distance $= \sqrt{(20 - 10)^2 + (8 - 5)^2} = \sqrt{10^2 + 3^2}$

$$= \sqrt{109} = 10.4 \, \text{unit}$$

15. $BD = 5 - 1.3 = 3.7m$

     (i)   (c) $\sin C = \dfrac{BD}{BC} = \dfrac{3.7}{7.4} = \dfrac{1}{2}$

        $\Rightarrow \quad \sin C = \sin 30° \Rightarrow \angle C = 30°$

     (ii)   (a) $\angle D + \angle B + \angle C = 180°$

        $\Rightarrow \quad 90° + \angle B + 30° = 180°$

        $\Rightarrow \quad \angle B = 60°$

     (iii)   (b) $\tan 30° = \dfrac{BD}{CD}$

$$\Rightarrow \frac{1}{\sqrt{3}} = \frac{3.7}{CD}$$

$$\Rightarrow CD = 3.7\sqrt{3}\,m$$

(iv) (d) $\sin B = \sin 60° = \dfrac{\sqrt{3}}{2}$

(v) (a) $\sin^2 B + \sin^2 C = \sin^2 60° + \sin^2 30°$

$$= \frac{3}{4} + \frac{1}{4} = 1$$

16. (i) (a) Area of field graze $= \dfrac{1}{4} \times \pi r^2$

$$= \frac{1}{4} \times 3.14 \times 5^2 = 19.625\,m^2$$

(ii) (b) Area of field graze $= \dfrac{1}{4} \times \pi r^2$

$$= \frac{1}{4} \times 3.14 \times 10^2 = 78.5\,m^2$$

(iii) (a) Increase in the grazing area
$= 78.5 - 19.625 = 58.875\,m^2$

(iv) (c) Area of square field $= 15 \times 15 = 225\,m^2$
Area of field not graze $= 225 - 19.625$
$= 205.37\,m^2$

(v) (a) Area of field not graze
$= 225 - 78.5 = 146.5\,m^2$

17. (i) (b)

(ii) (d)

(iii) (b)

(iv) (c) $PQ = 10 - 6 = 4\,m$

(v) (a) Area of $\triangle ABC = \dfrac{1}{2} \times 4 \times 6 = 12\,m^2$

18. $\because$ $500, 550, 600 \ldots\ldots$ are in A.P.

$\therefore$ $a = 500,\ d = 550 - 500 = 50$

(i) (a) $a_{18} = 500 + (18 - 1)50 = ₹1350$

(ii) (b) $a_n = 500 + (n - 1)50 = 500 + 50n - 50$
$= 450 + 50n = ₹50(n + 9)$

(iii) (a) $S_{20} = \dfrac{20}{2}[2 \times 500 + (20 - 1)50]$

$\qquad = 10[1950] = ₹19500$

(iv) (d) $S_n = \dfrac{n}{2}[1000 + (n - 1)50]$

$\qquad\qquad = \dfrac{n}{2}[950 + 50n] = ₹\dfrac{50n}{2}(n + 19)$

(v) (c)

19. (i) (a) Area of $\triangle ABC = \dfrac{\sqrt{3}}{4}a^2$

$\qquad\qquad 17320.5 = \dfrac{\sqrt{3}}{4}a^2$

$\qquad\qquad a^2 = \dfrac{17320.5 \times 4}{1.73205} = 40000$

$\qquad\qquad a = 200 \text{ cm}$

(ii) (d) Radius of circle $= \dfrac{200}{2}$

$\qquad\qquad = 100 \text{ cm}$

(iii) (a) Area of each sector

$\qquad\qquad = \dfrac{60}{360} \times \pi r^2$

$\qquad\qquad = \dfrac{1}{6} \times 3.14 \times 10000 = 5233.3 \text{ cm}^2$

(iv) (b) Area of the shaded region

$\qquad\qquad = $ Area of $\triangle ABC - 3 \times$ Area of each sector

$\qquad\qquad = 17320.5 - 3 \times \dfrac{31400}{6} = 1620.5 \text{ cm}^2$

(v) (c) Perimeter of $\triangle ABC = 3 \times 200 = 600 \text{ cm}$

20. (i) (b)

Let breadth of the rectangular park be x m.

$\therefore$ Length $= (x + 4)$m

Area of rectangular park $= x(x + 4)\text{m}^2$

Area of triangle $= \dfrac{1}{2} \times x \times 12 = 6x \text{ m}^2$

A.T.Q.

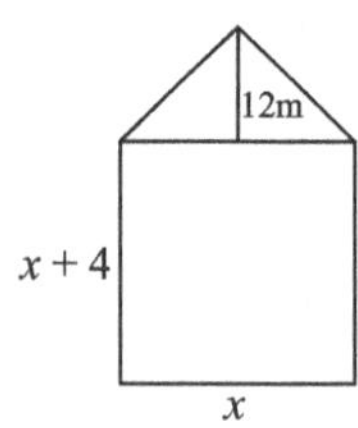

$$x(x+4) = 6x + 80$$
$$x^2 - 2x + 80 = 0$$
$$\Rightarrow \quad (x-10)(x+8) = 0$$
$$\Rightarrow \quad x = 10, -8$$
$$\therefore \quad \text{Breadth} = 10\,\text{m}$$

(ii) (c) Length $= x + 4$
$$= 10 + 4 = 14\,\text{m}$$

(iii) (b) Area of rectangular part $= x(x+4)$
$$= 10 \times 14 = 140\,\text{m}^2$$

(iv) (a) Area of triangular part $= 6x = 60\,\text{m}^2$

(v) (a) Area of park $= 140 + 60 = 200\,\text{m}^2$

21. (i) (b) Diameter of circle $= 2 \times 7 = 14$ cm

$\therefore$ length of side of square $= 3 \times 14 = 42$ cm

(ii) (a) Area of square $= 42 \times 42 = 1764\,\text{cm}^2$

(iii) (c) Diagonal of square $= \sqrt{2} \times$ side

$$= 42\sqrt{2}\ \text{cm}$$

(iv) (b) Area of each circular design $= \pi r^2$

$$= \frac{22}{7} \times 7 \times 7 = 154\,\text{cm}^2$$

(v) (a) Area of the remaining portion.
$$= \text{Area of square} - 9 \times \text{Area of circle}$$
$$= 1764 - 9 \times 154 = 378\ \text{cm}^2$$

22. (i) (c) $\because$ 20, 19, 18 .... are in A.P.

$\therefore a = 20, d = -1$ and $S_n = 200$

$$S_n = \frac{n}{2}[2a + (n-1)d]$$

$$200 = \frac{n}{2}[40 - (n-1)]$$

$$\Rightarrow n^2 - 4n + 400 = 0$$
$$\Rightarrow n = 25, 16.$$
$$\therefore n = 16$$

Number of rows $= 16$

(ii) (c) No. of log in top row

$$l = a + (n-1)d = 20 + 15\,(-1) = 5$$

(iii) (a) No. of log in 5th row from bottom

$$= 20 + 4\,(-1) = 16$$

(iv) (d) No. of log in 5th row from top

$$= 5 + 4\,(1) = 9$$

(v) (a) Difference between number of log in top and bottom $= 20 - 5 = 15$.

23. (i) (a) $\because$ Distance of the tower from B is twice its distance from A.

$$\therefore \text{PB} = 2\,\text{PA} \Rightarrow \frac{AP}{PB} = \frac{1}{2} = 1:2$$

(ii) (c)

(iii) (b) $P(x, y) = \left(\dfrac{36+0}{1+2}, \dfrac{15+0}{1+2} \right) = (12, 5)$

(iv) (a) $\because$ Coordinate of P(12, 5)

$$\therefore \text{AD} = 12$$

(v) (d) $PB = \sqrt{(36-12)^2 + (15-5)^2}$

$$= \sqrt{576 + 100} = 26$$

24. $\because$ $\triangle ABC \sim \triangle A'B'C'$

$$\therefore \quad \frac{AB}{A'B'} = \frac{BC}{B'C'} = \frac{AC}{A'C'} \qquad \text{...(i)}$$

and $\angle A = \angle A'$, $\angle B = \angle B'$, $\angle C = \angle C'$ ...(ii)

(i) (c) $\dfrac{AB}{A'B'} = \dfrac{AC}{A'C'} \Rightarrow \dfrac{5}{15} = \dfrac{3}{A'C'}$

$$\Rightarrow A'C' = 9\,\text{cm}$$

(ii) (a) $\dfrac{AB}{A'B'} = \dfrac{BC}{B'C'} \Rightarrow \dfrac{5}{15} = \dfrac{BC}{12}$

$$\Rightarrow BC = 4\,\text{cm}$$

(iii) (b) $\because \angle A = \angle A' = 80°$

(iv) (a) $\because \angle B = \angle B' = 60°$

(v) (b) $\because \angle A + \angle B + \angle C = 180°$

$$80° + 60° + \angle C = 180°$$
$$\angle C = 40°$$

25. (i) (b) Surface area of shed

$$= \text{Area of four walls} + \frac{1}{2} \text{ surface area of cylinder}$$

$$= 2h(l+b) + \frac{1}{2} \times 2\pi r(r+h)$$

$$= 2 \times 8(7+15) + \frac{1}{2} \times 2 \times \frac{22}{7} \times \frac{7}{2}\left(\frac{7}{2}+15\right)$$

$$= 555.5\,\text{m}^2$$

(ii) (c) Cost $= 555.5 \times 50 = ₹27775$

(iii) (a) Volume of air

$$= \text{Volume of cuboid} + \frac{1}{2} \times \text{Volume of cylinder}$$

$$= 8 \times 7 \times 15 + \frac{1}{2} \times \frac{22}{7} \times \frac{7}{2} \times \frac{7}{2} \times 15$$

$$= 1128.75\,\text{m}^3$$

(iv) (b) The total space occupied by the machinery $= 300\,\text{m}^3$

$\therefore$ Volume of air $= 1128.75 - 300$

$$= 828.75\,\text{m}^3$$

(v) (a) Volume of air for each worker

$$= \frac{828.75}{20} = 41.4375\,\text{m}^3.$$

26.   (i) (c) $\tan 30° = \dfrac{AB}{AC} \Rightarrow \dfrac{1}{\sqrt{3}} = \dfrac{20}{AC}$

$$AC = 20\sqrt{3}\,\text{m}$$

(ii) (b) $\sin 30° = \dfrac{AB}{BC} \Rightarrow \dfrac{1}{2} = \dfrac{20}{BC}$

$$BC = 40\,\text{m}$$

(iii) (a) $\angle B = 180 - (90+30°) = 60°$

(iv) (d) $\sin B - \sin C = \sin 60° - \sin 30°$

$$= \frac{\sqrt{3}}{2} - \frac{1}{2} = \frac{\sqrt{3}-1}{2}$$

(v) (b) $\sec^2 60° - \cot^2 30° = (2)^2 - \left(\sqrt{3}\right)^2 = 1$

27.   (i) (c) $AB = \sqrt{(2.4)^2 + (1.8)^2} = 3\,\text{m}.$

(ii) (b) $CD = 3.6 - 2.4 = 1.2\,\text{m}$

(iii) (a) $\because \triangle ABC \sim \triangle AEF$

$$\therefore \frac{AC}{AB} = \frac{AE}{AF}$$

$$\Rightarrow \quad \frac{1.8}{3} = \frac{0.9}{AF} \Rightarrow AF = 1.5 \text{ m}$$

(iv) (d)

(v) (a) Time $= \dfrac{D}{S} = \dfrac{300}{5} = 60 \text{ sec} = 1 \text{ min.}$

28. (i) (a) Distance run to pick up first potato

$\qquad = 3 + 3 = 6\text{m}$

(ii) (c) Distance run to pick up second potato

$\qquad = 6 + 2 + 2 = 10 \text{ m.}$

(iii) (b) Distance run to pick up 3rd potato.

$\qquad = 10 + 2 + 2 = 14 \text{ m.}$

(iv) (a) $\because$ 6, 10, 14 ..... are in AP.,

$\qquad \therefore d = 10 - 6 = 4 \text{ m}$

(v) (c) $S_{10} = \dfrac{10}{2}(2 \times 6 + 9 \times 4) = 240 \text{ m.}$

29. (i) (c) Let $AF = x$, then

$\qquad AE = AF = x$ [$\because$ tangents from point A]

$\qquad BF = BD = 6$ cm [tangents from point B]

$\qquad CE = CD = 8$ cm [tangents from point C]

$\qquad AB = AF + FB = x + 6$

$\qquad BC = BD + DC = 6 + 8 = 14$

$\qquad AC = AE + EC = x + 8$

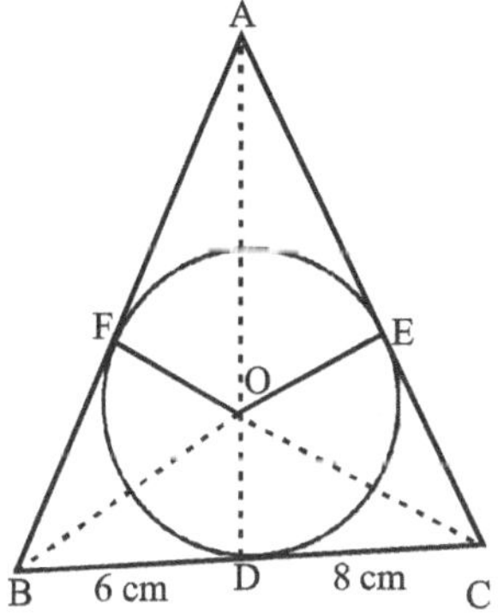

$$\text{Semiperimeter (s)} = \frac{AB + BC + CA}{2}$$

$$= x + 14$$

Area of $\triangle ABC$ = Area $(\triangle OBC)$ +
Area $(\triangle OCA)$ + Area $(\triangle AB)$

$$\sqrt{s(s-a)(s-b)(s-c)}$$

$$=\frac{1}{2}\times 14\times 4+\frac{1}{2}(x+8)\times 4+\frac{1}{2}(x+6)x$$

$$\sqrt{48x(x+14)}=4x+56$$

$$48x(x+14)=[4(x+14)]^2$$

$$3x=x+14 \Rightarrow x=7$$

$$\therefore \text{Area}(\triangle ABC)=\sqrt{48\times 7(7+14)}$$

$$=84\ \text{cm}^2$$

(ii) (c) $AC = x+8 = 7+8 = 15\ \text{cm}$

(iii) (b) $AB = AF+FB = x+6 = 7+6 = 13\ \text{cm}$

(iv) (a)   Perimeter of triangle $(\triangle ABC)$

   $=AB+BC+AC$

   $=13+14+15=42\ \text{cm}$

(v) (a)   By Pythagoras theorem in right $\triangle ODC$,

   $OC^2 = OD^2 + DC^2 = 4^2 + 8^2$ $[\because \text{radius}=OD=4\ \text{cm}]$

   $=16+64=80$

   $OC = \sqrt{80}=4\sqrt{5}\ \text{cm}$

30. (i)   (b)   Number rungs in the ladder (n)

$$=\frac{\text{Length between top and bottom rungs}}{\text{Length between any two rungs}}$$

$$=\frac{2\frac{2}{2}\text{m}}{25\text{cm}}=\frac{250}{25}=10$$

(ii) (a)   Since, length of rungs of are decreasing uniformly

So, length of rungs form an A.P.

First term (a) = Length of bottom rung = 45 cm

Last term $(a_n = l)$ = Length of top rung = 25 cm

Number of rungs (n) = 10

$$\text{Common difference (d)} = \frac{l-a}{n-1}=\frac{25-45}{10-1}$$

$$=-\frac{20}{9}=-2.22\text{cm}$$

$\therefore$ Rungs are uniformly decreasing by length

$= 2.22$ cm

(iii) (a)   Length of 7th rung $= 45 + (7-1)(-2.22)$

$= 45 - 13.32$

$= 31.68$ cm.

(iv) (a)   Length of wood required for rungs

$$= \frac{n}{2}[a+l] = \frac{10}{2}[45+25]$$

$= 5 \times 70 = 350$ cm.

(v) (d)   Length of 4th rung

$= 45 + 3(-2.22)$ $[\because a_n = a + (n-1)d]$

$= 38.84$ cm.

Difference of length of 4th and 7th rungs

$= 38.34 - 31.68 = 6.66$ cm.

31. (i) (c)   Volume of spherical $= \dfrac{4}{3}\pi r^3$

(ii) (c)   Diameter of cylindrical part

$$= \frac{2}{5} \times 10 = 4 \text{cm}$$

$\therefore$ Radius of cylindrical part

$$= \frac{4}{2} = 2 \text{cm}$$

(iii) (b)   Radius of spherical part

$$= \frac{10}{2} = 5 \text{cm}$$

$\therefore$ Volume of spherical part

$$= \frac{4}{3}\pi r^3 = \frac{4}{3} \times 3.14 \times (5)^3$$

$$= \frac{4}{3} \times 3.14 \times 125 = 523.33 \text{ cm}^3$$

(iv) (a)   Volume of cylindrical neck $= \pi r^2 h$

$= 3.14 \times (2)^2 \times 8$

$= 3.14 \times 4 \times 8 = 100.48 \text{ cm}^3$

(v) (d)   Total volume of solid figure

$= 523.33 + 100.48 = 623.81 \text{ cm}^3$

32. (i) (a) In $\triangle ABD$,

$$\tan 30° = \frac{AB}{BD} \Rightarrow \frac{1}{\sqrt{3}} = \frac{20}{BD}$$

$$\Rightarrow BD = 20\sqrt{3} \Rightarrow 34.64 \text{ m}$$

(ii) (c) $\tan 60° = \dfrac{BC}{BD}$

$$\Rightarrow \sqrt{3} = \frac{AB + AC}{20\sqrt{3}}$$

$$20 + AC = 60$$

$$AC = 60 - 20 = 40 \text{ m}$$

(iii) (a) Difference of length of flag staff and wall

$$= 40 - 20 = 20 \text{ m}$$

(iv) (a) $4 \sin \angle ADB + 3 \cos \angle BDC$

$$= 4 \sin 30° + 3 \cos 60°$$

$$= 4 \times \frac{1}{2} + 3 \times \frac{1}{2}$$

$$= \frac{4}{2} + \frac{3}{2} = \frac{7}{2}$$

(v) (d) In $\triangle ABD$, Pythagoras theorem

$$AD^2 = AB^2 + BD^2$$

$$= (20)^2 + \left(20\sqrt{3}\right)^2 = 400 + 400 \times 3$$

$$= 1600 = 4 \times 4 \times 10 \times 10$$

$$\Rightarrow AD = 40 \text{ m}.$$

33. (i) (c) In $\triangle APB$

$$\tan 30° = \frac{AB}{AP} \Rightarrow \frac{1}{\sqrt{3}} = \frac{10}{AP}$$

$$\Rightarrow \quad AP = 10\sqrt{3} = 10 \times 1.732 = 17.32 \text{ m}.$$

(ii) (a) In $\triangle APB$

$$\sin 30° = \frac{AB}{PB}$$

$$\Rightarrow \quad \frac{1}{2} = \frac{10}{PB}$$

$$\Rightarrow \quad PB = 20 \text{ m}.$$

(iii) (b) In $\triangle APD$

$$\tan 45° = \frac{AD}{AP} \Rightarrow 1 = \frac{AD}{10\sqrt{3}}$$

$\Rightarrow \quad AD = 10\sqrt{3}$ m.

Height of the flagstaff $= AD - AB$

$$= 10\sqrt{3} - 10 = 10(\sqrt{3} - 1)$$

$$= 10(1.732 - 1) = 7.32 \text{ m.}$$

(iv) (a) In $\triangle APD$

$$\sin 45° = \frac{AD}{PD} \Rightarrow \frac{1}{\sqrt{2}} = \frac{10\sqrt{3}}{PD}$$

$\Rightarrow \quad PD = 10\sqrt{6}$ m.

(v) (c) Ratio $= \dfrac{7.32}{10} = \dfrac{732}{1000} = \dfrac{183}{250}$

$$= 183 : 250$$

34. (i) (b) Surface area of hemisphere $= 2\pi r^2$

$$= 2 \times \frac{22}{7} \times 3.5 \times 3.5 = 77 \text{ cm}^2$$

(ii) (a) C.S.A of cylinder $= 2\pi rh$

$$= 2 \times \frac{22}{7} \times 3.5 \times 10 = 220 \text{ cm}^2$$

(iii) (c) Total surface area of the article
$= 220 + 2 \times 77 = 374 \text{ cm}^2$

(iv) (b) Volume of hemisphere $= \dfrac{2}{3}\pi r^3$

$$= \frac{2}{3} \times \frac{22}{7} \times 3.5 \times 3.5 \times 3.5$$

$$= 89.83 \text{ cm}^3$$

(v) (a) Volume of articles
$= $ Volume of cylinder $- 2 \times$ Volume of hemisphere
$= \pi r^2 h - 2 \times 89.83$

$$= \frac{22}{7} \times 3.5 \times 3.5 \times 10 - 2 \times 89.83$$

$$= 385 - 179.66 = 205.34 \, \text{cm}^3$$

35. (i) (a) Radius of inner semicircular end

$$= \frac{60}{2} = 30 \, \text{m}$$

(ii) (c) Radius of outer semicircular end

$$= 30 + 10 = 40 \, \text{m}$$

(iii) (b) The distance arounded the track along its inner edge $= 106 \times 2 + 2 \times \pi r$

$$= 212 + 2 \times \frac{22}{7} \times 30 = 212 + 188.57$$

$$= 400.57 \, \text{m}$$

(iv) (d) The distance arounded the track along its outer edge

$$= 106 \times 2 + 2 \times \pi r$$

$$= 212 + 2 \times \frac{22}{7} \times 40 = 212 + 251.43$$

$$= 463.43 \, \text{m}$$

(v) (a) The area of the track

$$= 2 \times \text{Area of ractangle} + 2 \times \text{Area of semicircular ring.}$$

$$= 2(10 \times 106) + 2 \times \frac{1}{2} \times \frac{22}{7} \times (40^2 - 30^2)$$

$$= 2120 + 2200 = 4320 \, \text{m}^2$$

36. (i) (c) A $(2, 3)$

(ii) (a) B $(-2, 0)$

(iii) (c) $AB = \sqrt{(2+2) + (3-0)^2} = \sqrt{16+9}$

$$= 5 \, \text{cm}^2$$

(iv) (b) C $(3, 0)$

(v) (a) Mid-point of B and C

$$\left(\frac{3 + (-2)}{2}, \frac{0+0}{2} \right) = \left(\frac{5}{2}, 0 \right)$$

37. (i) (c) Height of cylinder $= 10 - 3 = 7 \, \text{m}$

(ii) (a) Radius of hemisphere $= \dfrac{3}{2} = 1.5 \, \text{m.}$

(iii) (b) Surface area of container

$$= 2 \times \frac{22}{7} \times 1.5 \times 7 + 2 \times 2 \times \frac{22}{7} \times 1.5 \times 1.5$$

$$= 66 + 28.29 = 94.29 \, m^2$$

(iv) (c) Volume of oil $= \frac{22}{7} \times 1.5 \times 1.5 \times 7$

$$= \frac{22}{7} \times 1.5 \times 1.5 \times 7 + 2 \times \frac{2}{3} \times \frac{22}{7} \times 1.5 \times 1.5 \times 1.5$$

$$= 49.5 + 14.14 = 63.64 \, m^3.$$

(v) (d) Cost $= 63.64 \times 50 = ₹ 3182.$

38. (i) (a)

(ii) (b)

(iii) (a) $a_n = 3 + (n-1)3 = 3n$

(iv) (c) $a_{11} = 3 \times 11 = 33$

(v) (b) $a_7 = (7)^2 = 49.$

39. (i) (c) $\because$ ΔOAB is equilateral triangle

$\therefore$ $AB = 5 \, cm.$

(ii) (b) Area of circle $= \frac{22}{7} \times 5 \times 5$

$$= 78.57 \, cm^2$$

(iii) (a) Area of minor sector

$$= \frac{60}{360} \times \frac{22}{7} \times 5 \times 5 = 13.09 \, cm^2$$

(iv) (a) Area of major sector

$$= 78.57 - 13.09 = 65.48 \, cm^2$$

(v) (b) Length of arc APB

$$= \frac{\theta}{360} \times 2\pi r = \frac{60}{360} \times 2 \times \frac{22}{7} \times 5$$

$$= 5.24 \, cm.$$

40. (i) (c) $A(2, 2)$

(ii) (a) $B(5, -2)$

(iii) (b) $AB = \sqrt{(2+2)^2 + (2-5)^2}$

$$= \sqrt{16+9} = 5 \, unit$$

(iv) (c) $C(k, 0) = \dfrac{k(5)+2}{k+1}, \dfrac{k(-2)+2}{k+1}$

$$0 = \dfrac{-2k+2}{k+1} \quad \Rightarrow \quad k = 1 : 1$$

(v) (a) $OB = \sqrt{5^2 + (-2)^2} = \sqrt{25+4}$

$$= \sqrt{29} \text{ unit}$$

41. (i) (d)

   (ii) (b)

   (iii) (c)   AAA is not a congruence rule.

   (iv) (a)

   (v) (b)

42. (i) (a)   Sum of zeroes $= -\dfrac{\text{coefficient of } x}{\text{coefficient of } x^2}$

$$= -\dfrac{(-12)}{4} = 3$$

   (ii) (d)   Product of zeroes $= \dfrac{\text{constant term}}{\text{coefficient of } x^2}$

$$= \dfrac{c}{a}$$

   (iii) (c) $\because$ One zero of the polynomial is four times the other

$$\therefore \beta = 4\alpha$$

   (iv) (d) $\alpha + \beta = -\dfrac{b}{a} = 3$

$$\Rightarrow \quad \alpha + \beta = 3$$
$$\Rightarrow \quad \alpha + 4\alpha = 3 \quad [\because \beta = 4\alpha]$$

$$\Rightarrow \quad \alpha = \dfrac{3}{5}$$

   (v) (b) $\because \alpha\beta = \dfrac{3k+8}{4}$

$$\alpha \cdot (4\alpha) = \dfrac{3k+8}{4} \quad [\because \beta = 4\alpha]$$

$$4\alpha^2 = \dfrac{3k+8}{4}$$

$$4\left(\frac{3}{5}\right)^2 = \frac{36}{25} = \frac{3k+8}{4}$$

$$\Rightarrow \quad 144 = 75k + 200$$

$$\Rightarrow \quad k = \frac{144 - 200}{75} = -\frac{56}{75}$$

$$\therefore \quad k = -\frac{56}{75}$$

43. (i) (d) Area of circle $= \pi r^2$

(ii) (a) Area of sector of circle $= \pi r^2 \cdot \dfrac{\theta}{360°}$

(iii) (a) Area of major sector

$$= \text{Area of circle} - \text{Area of minor sector}$$

$$= \pi r^2 - \pi r^2 \frac{\theta}{360°}$$

$$= \pi r^2 \left(\frac{360° - \theta}{360}\right)$$

$$= \frac{22}{7} \times (21)^2 \left(\frac{360 - 90°}{360}\right)$$

$$= 1386 \times \frac{270°}{360°}$$

$$= 1386 \times 0.75 = 1039.5 \text{ cm}^2$$

(iv) (c) Area of minor segment

$$= \text{Area of minor sector} - \text{Area of triangle}$$

$$= \pi r^2 \frac{\theta}{360°} - \frac{1}{2} OA \times OB$$

$$= \frac{22}{7} \times (21)^2 \frac{90°}{360} - \frac{1}{2} \times 21 \times 21$$

$$= \frac{21 \times 21}{2} \left[\frac{11}{7} - 1\right]$$

$$= 126 \text{ cm}^2$$

(v) (b) Area of major segment

$= \pi r^2 -$ Area of minor segment

$= \dfrac{22}{7} \times 21 \times 21 - 126$

$= 1386 - 126$

$= 1260 \, \text{cm}^2$

44. (i) (b) $QS = PS - PQ = 6 - 1.5 = 4.5 \, \text{m}$

(ii) (c) $\tan 60° = \dfrac{QS}{SR}$

$\sqrt{3} = \dfrac{4.5}{SR}$

$\Rightarrow \quad SR = \dfrac{4.5}{\sqrt{3}} \approx 2.6 \, \text{m (approx)} \; [1 \text{ Mark}]$

(iii) (a) $\sin 60° = \dfrac{QS}{QR}$

$\dfrac{\sqrt{3}}{2} = \dfrac{4.5}{QR}$

$\Rightarrow \quad QR = \dfrac{4.5 \times 2}{\sqrt{3}} = 5.19 \, \text{m}$

$\therefore$ Length of ladder is $5.19 \, \text{m}$.

(iv) (a) $\tan 45° = \dfrac{QS}{SR}$

$1 = \dfrac{QS}{SR}$

$QS = SR$

(v) (a)

Latest Revised Syllabus Issued by CBSE for Academic Year (2020-2021)

SOCIAL SCIENCE CLASS X (2020-21)

Theory Paper
Time: 3 Hours   **Max. Marks: 80**

No.	Units	No. of Periods	Marks
I	India and the Contemporary World-II	46	20
II	Contemporary India - II	34	20
III	Democratic Politics-II	27	20
IV	Understanding Economic Development	44	20
	TOTAL	151	80

Unit 1: India and the Contemporary World-II   **46 Periods**

Themes	Learning Objectives
Section 1: Events and Processes:	
1. The Rise of Nationalism in Europe: • The French Revolution and the Idea of the Nation • The Making of Nationalism in Europe • The Age of Revolutions: 1830-1848 • The Making of Germany and Italy • Visualizing the Nation • Nationalism and Imperialism	• Enable the learners to identify and comprehend the forms in which nationalism developed along with the formation of nation states in Europe in the post-1830 period. • Establish the relationship and bring out the difference between European nationalism and anti-colonial nationalisms. • Understand the way the idea of nationalism emerged and led to the formation of nation states in Europe and elsewhere.
2. Nationalism in India: • The First World War, Khilafat and Non - Cooperation • Differing Strands within the Movement • Towards Civil Disobedience • The Sense of Collective Belonging	• Recognize the characteristics of Indian nationalism through a case study of Non-Cooperation and Civil Disobedience Movement. • Analyze the nature of the diverse social movements of the time. • Familiarize with the writings and ideals of different political groups and individuals. • Appreciate the ideas promoting Pan Indian belongingness.

Themes	Learning Objectives
Section 2: Livelihoods, Economies and Societies: Any one theme of the following:	
3. The Making of a Global World: • The Pre-modern world • The Nineteenth Century (1815-1914) • The Inter war Economy • Rebuilding a World Economy: The Post-War Era	• Show that globalization has a long history and point to the shifts within the process. • Analyze the implication of globalization for local economies. • Discuss how globalization is experienced differently by different social groups.
4. The Age of Industrialization: • Before the Industrial Revolution • Hand Labour and Steam Power • Industrialization in the colonies • Factories Come Up • The Peculiarities of Industrial Growth • Market for Goods	• Familiarize with the Proto Industrial Phase and Early factory system. • Familiarize with the process of industrialization and its impact on labour class. • Enable them to understand industrialization in the colonies with reference to Textile industries.
Unit 2 : Contemporary India - II	**34 Periods**
1. Resources and Development: • Types of Resources • Development of Resources • Resource Planning in India • Land Resources • Land Utilization • Land Use Pattern in India • Land Degradation and Conservation Measures • Soil as a Resource • Classification of Soils • Soil Erosion and Soil Conservation **Note:** *The chapter 'Forest and Wildlife' to be assessed in the Periodic Tests only and will not be evaluated in Board Examination.*	• Understand the value of resources and the need for their judicious utilization and conservation.
3. Water Resources: **Note:** *The theoretical aspects of this chapter will not be assessed in periodic tests and Board Examination. Only map items as given in the map list from this chapter will be evaluated in the Board Examination.*	• Identify different dams in the country.
4. Agriculture: • Types of farming • Cropping Pattern • Major Crops • Technological and Institutional Reforms • Impact of Globalization on Agriculture	• Explain the importance of agriculture in national economy. • Identify various types of farming and discuss the various farming methods; describe the spatial distribution of major crops as well as understand the relationship between rainfall regimes and cropping pattern. • Explain various government policies for institutional as well as technological reforms since independence.

<table>
<tr><th align="center">Themes</th><th align="center">Learning Objectives</th></tr>
<tr><td>

5. Minerals and Energy Resources
Note: *The theoretical aspects of this chapter will not be assessed in periodic tests and Board Examination. Only map items as given in the map list from this chapter will be evaluated in the Board Examination.*

</td><td>

- Identify places of availability of different energy resources.

</td></tr>
<tr><td>

6. Manufacturing Industries:
- Importance of manufacturing
- Contribution of Industry to National Economy
- Industrial Location
- Classification of Industries
- Spatial distribution
- Industrial pollution and environmental degradation
- Control of Environmental Degradation

</td><td>

- Bring out the importance of industries in the national economy as well as understand the regional disparities which resulted due to concentration of industries in some areas.
- Discuss the need for a planned industrial development and debate over the role of government towards sustainable development.

</td></tr>
<tr><td>

7. Life Lines of National Economy:
- Transport – Roadways, Railways, Pipelines, Waterways, Airways
- Communication
- International Trade
- Tourism as a Trade

</td><td>

- Explain the importance of transport and communication in the ever-shrinking world.
- Understand the role of trade and tourism in the economic development of a country.

</td></tr>
<tr><td colspan="2">

Unit 3 : Democratic Politics –II   **27 Periods**

</td></tr>
<tr><td>

1.   Power Sharing:
- Case Studies of Belgium and Sri Lanka
- Why power sharing is desirable?
- Forms of Power Sharing

</td><td>

- Familiarize with the centrality of power sharing in a democracy.
- Understand the working of spatial and social power sharing mechanisms.

</td></tr>
<tr><td>

2.   Federalism:
- What is Federalism?
- What make India a Federal Country?
- How is Federalism practiced?
- Decentralization in India

</td><td>

- Analyse federal provisions and institutions.
- Explain decentralization in rural and urban areas.

</td></tr>
<tr><td>

6.   Political Parties:
- Why do we need Political Parties?
- How many Parties should we have?
- National Political Parties
- State Parties
- Challenges to Political Parties
- How can Parties be reformed?

</td><td>

- Analyse party systems in democracies.
- Introduction to major political parties, challenges faced by them and reforms in the country.

</td></tr>
</table>

Themes	Learning Objectives
7. Outcomes of Democracy: • How do we assess democracy's outcomes? • Accountable, responsive and legitimate government • Economic growth and development • Reduction of inequality and poverty • Accommodation of social diversity • Dignity and freedom of the citizens	• Evaluate the functioning of democracies in comparison to alternative forms of governments. • Understand the causes for continuation of democracy in India. • Distinguish between sources of strengths and weaknesses of Indian democracy.

Unit 4 : Understanding Economic Development	**44 Periods**

Themes	Learning Objectives
1. Development: • What Development Promises - Different people different goals • Income and other goals • National Development • How to compare different countries or states? • Income and other criteria • Public Facilities • Sustainability of development	• Familiarize with concepts of macroeconomics. • Understand the rationale for overall human development in our country, which includes the rise of income, improvements in health and education rather than income. • Understand the importance of quality of life and sustainable development.
2. Sectors of the Indian Economy: • Sectors of Economic Activities • Comparing the three sectors • Primary, Secondary and Tertiary Sectors in India • Division of sectors as organized and unorganized • Sectors in terms of ownership: Public and Private Sectors	• Identify major employment generating sectors. • Reason out the government investment in different sectors of economy.
3. Money and Credit: • Money as a medium of exchange • Modern forms of money • Loan activities of Banks • Two different credit situations • Terms of credit • Formal sector credit in India • Self Help Groups for the Poor	• Understand money as an economic concept. • Understand the role of financial institutions from the point of view of day-to- day life.
4. Globalization and the Indian Economy: • Production across countries • Interlinking production across countries • Foreign Trade and integration of markets • What is globalization? • Factors that have enabled Globalisation • World Trade Organisation • Impact of Globalization on India • The Struggle for a fair Globalisation	• Explain the working of the Global Economic phenomenon.

CBSE Sample Paper 2021

INSTRUCTION: Question 1 to 44 are case based questions. Attempt any 4 sub parts. Each question carry 1 mark.

1. **Read the source given below and answer the questions that follows:**

   Following the defeat of Napoleon in 1815, European governments were driven by a spirit of conservatism. Conservatives believed that established, traditional institutions of state and society – like the monarchy, the Church, social hierarchies, property and the family – should be preserved. Most conservatives, however, did not propose a return to the society of pre-revolutionary days. Rather, they realised, from the changes initiated by Napoleon, that modernisation could in fact strengthen traditional institutions like the monarchy. It could make state power more effective and stronger. A modern army, an efficient bureaucracy, a dynamic economy, the abolition of feudalism and serfdom could strengthen the autocratic monarchies of Europe. In 1815, representatives of European powers who had collectively defeated Napoleon, met at Vienna to draw up a settlement for Europe. The Congress was hosted by the Austrian Chancellor Duke Metternich. The delegates drew up the Treaty of Vienna of 1815 with the object of undoing most of the changes the had come about in Europe during the Napoleonic wars. The Bourbon dynasty, which had been deposed during the French Revolution, was restored to power, and France lost the territories it had annexed under Napoleon. A series of states were set up on the boundaries of France to prevent French expansion in future.

Answer the following MCQs by choosing the most appropriate option

1.1 Which of the following statements correctly describes about European conservative ideology?

   (a) Preservation of believes introduced by Napoleon

   (b) Preservation of two sects of Christianity

   (c) Preservation of socialist ideology in economic sphere

   (d) Preservation of traditionalist beliefs in state and society

1.2 Identify the purpose to convene the Vienna of Congress in 1815 from the following options?

   (a) To declare competition of German unification

   (b) To restore conservative regime in Europe

   (c) To decalre war against France

   (d) To start the process of Italian Unification

1.3 What did conservatives focus on at the Congress of Vienna? Select the appropriate option.

    (a) To re-established peace and stability in Europe

    (b) To establish socialism in Europe

    (c) To introduce democracy in France

    (d) To set up a new Parliament in Austria

1.4 How did the Congress of Vienna ensure peace in Europe? Select the appropriate option.

    (a) With the restoration of Bourbon Dynasty

    (b) Austria was not given the control of Northern Italy

    (c) Laying out a balance of power between all the great powers in Europe

    (d) By giving power to the German confederation

2. **Read the text given below and answer the following questions.**

Manufacturing industries not only help in modernising agriculture, which forms the backbone of our economy, they also reduce the heavy dependence of people on agricultural income by providing them jobs in secondary and tertiary sectors. Industrial developments is a precondition for eradication of unemployment and poverty from our country. This was the main philosophy behind public sector industries and joint sector ventures in India. It was also aimed at bringing down regional disparities by establishing industries in tribal and backward areas. Export of manufactured goods expands trade and commerce, and brings in much needed foreign exchange. Countries that transform their raw materials into a wide variety of finished goods of higher value are prosperous. India's prosperity lies in increasing and diversifying its manufacturing industries as quickly as possible. Agriculture and industry are not exclusive of each other. They move hand in hand. For instance, the agro-industries in India have given a major boost to agriculture by raising its productivity.

Answer the following MCQs by choosing the most appropriate option

2.1 Manufacturing industries fall in __________ and agriculture in __________.

    (a) Primary, Secondary Sector

    (b) Secondary, Tertiary Sector

    (c) Primary, Tertiary Sector

    (d) Secondary, Primary Sector

2.2 Manufacturing provides job opportunities to reduce dependence on agriculture. Identify which sector the following jobs belong to -

Jobs created or promoted by manufacturing industries	Sector
a. Garment production	1. Primary
b. Research & Development	2. Tertiary

c. Banking	3. Secondary
d. Mining	4. Quaternary

Choose the correct option -

(a) a-1, b-2, c-3, d-4

(b) a-3, b-4, c-2, d-1

(c) a-2, b-3, c-1, d-2

(d) a-4, b-1, c-4, d-3

2.3 Which of the following options does not help in modernising agriculture?

(a) Manufacturing farm equipment

(b) Providing unskilled labour force

(c) Supplying fertilizers and pesticides

(d) Producing tube well pumps and sprinklers

2.4 In order to attract foreign manufacturing firms, a country needs to develop -

(a) Agrarian facilities

(b) Cultivable lands

(c) Media facilities

(d) Infrastructure facilities

3. **Read the given extract and answer the following questions.**

In a democracy, we are most concerned with ensuring that people will have the right to choose their rulers and people will have control over the rulers. Whenever possible and necessary, citizens should be able to participate in decision making, that affects them all. Therefore, the most basic outcome of democracy should be that it produces a government that is accountable to the citizens, and responsive to the needs and expectations of the citizens. Some people think that democracy produces less effective government. It is, of course, true that non-democratic rulers are very quick and efficient in decision making and implementation, whereas, democracy is based on the idea of deliberation and negotiation. So, some delay is bound to take place. But, because it has followed procedures, its decisions may be both more acceptable to the people and more effective. Moreover, when citizens want to know if a decision was taken through the correct procedures, they can find this out. They have the right and the means to examine the process of decision making. This is known as transparency. This factor is often missing from a non-democratic government. There is another aspect in which democratic government is certainly better than its alternatives: democratic government is legitimate government. It may be slow, less efficient, not always very responsive, or clean. But a democartic government is people's own government.

Answer the following MCQs by choosing the most appropriate option

3.1 People's right to choose their own rulers is called as the -

(a) Right to Initiate   (b) Right to Plebiscite

(c) Right to Vote   (d) Right to Referendum

3.2 Which of the following options helps in promoting transparency in the governance?

(a) Right to education

(b) Right to information

(c) Right to against exploitation

(d) Right to speech and expression

3.3 _____________________ make/s the government legitimate.

(a) Credibility of politicians

(b) People's movements

(c) Free and fair elections

(d) Holding of powers

3.4 Decisions in a democracy are more acceptable to the people because they are -

(a) Taken swiftly and implemented quickly

(b) Taken by giving privileges to the people

(c) Taken through elites' votes

(d) Taken after following due processes

4. **Read the source given below and answer the following questions -**

Ford Motors, an American company, is one of the world's largest automobile manufacturers with production spread over 26 countries of the world. Ford Motors came to India in 1995 and spent Rs. 1700 crore to set up a large plant near Chennai. This was done in collaboration with Mahindra and Mahindra, a major Indian manufacturer of jeeps and trucks. By the year 2004, Ford Motors was selling 27,000 cars in the Indian markets, while 24,000 cars were exported from India to South Africa, Mexico and Brazil. The company wanted to develop Ford India as a component supplying base for its other plants across the globe.

Answer the following MCQs by choosing the most appropriate option

4.1 The passage given above relates to which of the following options?

(a) Increased employment

(b) Foreign investment

(c) Foreign collaboration

(d) International competition

4.2   According to the given passage, Ford Motors can be termed as a Multi-National Company based on which of the following options?

(a) Production of different types of automobiles

(b) Largest automobile manufacturer in the world

(c) Because of largescale exports of cars across globe

(d) Industrial and commercial ventures across globe

4.3   By setting up their production plants in India, Ford Motors wanted to -

(a) Collaborate with a leading Indian Automobile company

(b) Satisfy the demands of American, African and Indian markets

(c) Tap the benefits of low-cost production and a large market

(d) Take over small automobile manufacturing units in India

4.4   'Ford Motors' wish to develop Ford India as a component supplying base for its other plants across the globe is an evidence of -

(a) Promoting local industries of India

(b) Merging trade from different countries

(c) Supplying jobs to factory workers in India

(d) Interlinking of production across countries

Practice Case Study MCQs

5.   **Read the source given below and answer the questions that follows:**

In the seventeenth and eighteenth centuries, merchants from the towns in Europe began moving to the countryside, supplying money to peasants and artisans, persuading them to produce for an international market. With the expansion of world trade and the acquisition of colonies in different parts of the world, the demand for goods began growing. But merchants could not expand production within towns. This was because here urban crafts and trade guilds were powerful. These were associations of producers that trained craftspeople, maintained control over production, regulated competition and prices, and restricted the entry of new people into the trade. Rulers granted different guilds the monopoly right to produce and trade in specific products. It was therefore difficult for new merchants to set up business in towns. So they turned to the countryside.

5.1   Merchants persuaded the artisans to produce for the

(a) Poor peasants   (b) Local Markets   (c) Self-sufficiency   (d) International Markets

5.2   Which of the following was/were the reason(s) for increase in demand of goods?

(a) Acquisition of colonies   (b) Expansion of world trade

(c) Mass Production   (d) Both a and b

5.3　consider the following statements:

1. Merchants could not expand production within towns.

2. This was because here urban crafts and trade guilds were powerful.

Which of the statement(s) given above is/are correct?

(a) 1 only　　　　(b) 2 only　　　　(c) Both 1 and 2　　　　(d) Neither 1 nor 2

5.4　Which of the following was the reason for merchants turning to countryside?

(a)　Lack of resources　　　　(b) Monopoly rights given to guilds

(c)　Poor environment of towns　　　　(d) High labour cost

6.　**Read the text given below and answer the following questions**

We have shared our land with the past generations and will have to do so with the future generations too. Ninety-five per cent of our basic needs for food, shelter and clothing are obtained from land. Human activities have not only brought about degradation of land but have also aggravated the pace of natural forces to cause damage to land. At present, there are about 130 million hectares of degraded land in India. Approximately, 28 per cent of it belongs to the category of forest degraded area, 56 per cent of it is water eroded area and the rest is affected by saline and alkaline deposits. Some human activities such as deforestation, over grazing, mining and quarrying too have contributed significantly in land degradation. Mining sites are abandoned after excavation work is complete leaving deep scars and traces of over-burdening. In states like Jharkhand, Chhattisgarh, Madhya Pradesh and Odisha deforestation due to mining have caused severe land degradation.

6.1　_________ per cent of our basic needs for food, shelter and clothing are obtained from land.

(a) 70　　　　(b) 85　　　　(c) 95　　　　(d) 100

6.2　At present, about how many million hectares of degraded land is there in India?

(a) 125　　　　(b) 130　　　　(c) 150　　　　(d) 100

6.3　The highest percentage of degraded land is by which factor?

(a) Deforestation　　　(b) Water　　　　(c) Salinity　　　　(d) Alkalinity

6.4　In states like Jharkhand, Chhattisgarh, Madhya Pradesh and Odisha deforestation due to _________ have caused severe land degradation.

(a) mining　　　　(b) grazing　　　　(c) flooding　　　　(d) Urbanisation

7.　**Read the given extract and answer the following questions**

Over a hundred countries of the world today claim and practice some kind of democratic politics: they have formal constitutions, they hold elections, they have parties and they guarantee rights of citizens. While these features are common to most of them, these democracies are very much different from each other in terms of their social situations, their economic achievements and their cultures. Clearly, what may be achieved or not achieved under each of these democracies will be very different. But is there something that we can expect from every democracy, just because it is democracy? Our interest in and fascination for democracy often pushes us into taking a position that democracy can address all socio-economic and political problems. If some of our expectations are not met, we start blaming the idea of democracy. Or, we start doubting if we are living in a democracy. The first step towards thinking carefully about the outcomes of democracy is to recognise that democracy is just a form of government. It can only create conditions for achieving something. The citizens have to take advantage of those conditions and achieve those goals.

7.1 _______countries of the world today claim and practice some kind of democratic politics.

(a) More than 100

(b) More than 50 but less than 100

(c) More than 200

(d) Less than 50

7.2 The countries practising democracy have

(a) Same culture

(b) Same Social Structure

(c) Similar Economies

(d) None of the above

7.3 Consider the following statements:

1. What may be achieved or not achieved under democracies will be very different.

2. Democracy cannot address all the problems of society.

Which of the statement(s) given above is/are correct?

(a) 1 only   (b) 2 only   (c) 1 & 2 only   (d) Neither 1 nor 2

7.4 According to the passage, which of the following are associated with democracy?

1. Holding elections   2. Formal Constitution 3. Rights   4. Caste Reservations

Select the correct answer using the codes given below:

(a) 1 and 2 only   (b) 2 and 4 only   (c) 1, 2 and 3 only   (d) All of the above

8. **Read the source given below and answer the following questions**

Generally, it has been noted from the histories of many, now developed, countries that at initial stages of development, primary sector was the most important sector of economic activity. As the methods of farming changed and agriculture sector began to prosper, it produced much more food than before. Many people could now take up other activities. There were increasing number of craftpersons and traders. Buying and selling activities increased many times. Besides, there were also transporters, administrators, army etc. However, at this stage, most of the goods produced were natural products from the primary sector and most people were also employed in this sector. Over a long time (more than hundred years), and especially because new methods of manufacturing were introduced, factories came up and started expanding. Those people who had earlier worked on farms now began to work in factories in large numbers. People began to use many more goods that were produced in factories at cheap rates. Secondary sector gradually became the most important in total production and employment. Hence, over time, a shift had taken place. This means that the importance of the sectors had changed.

8.1 At initial stages of development, which sector is the most important sector of economic activity?

    (a) Primary   (b) Secondary   (c) Tertiary   (d) Quaternary

8.2 Agricultural prosperity leads to which of the following?

    (a) Increased buying and selling   (b) Growth in number of craftsperson

    (c) Production of much more food grains   (d) All of the above

8.3 In primary sector most of the goods produced are

    (a) Natural   (b) Synthetic   (c) Artificial   (d) None of the above

8.4 Those people who had earlier worked on farms now began to work in __________ in large numbers.

    (a) Factories   (b) Railways   (c) Towns   (d) Villages

9.   **Read the source given below and answer the questions that follows:**

Ideas of national unity in early-nineteenth-century Europe were closely allied to the ideology of liberalism. The term 'liberalism' derives from the Latin root liber, meaning free. For the new middle classes liberalism stood for freedom for the individual and equality of all before the law. Politically, it emphasised the concept of government by consent. Since the French Revolution, liberalism had stood for the end of autocracy and clerical privileges, a constitution and representative government through parliament. Nineteenth-century liberals also stressed the inviolability of private property. Yet, equality before the law did not necessarily stand for universal suffrage. You will recall that in revolutionary France, which marked the first political experiment in liberal democracy, the right to vote and to get elected was granted exclusively to property-owning men. Men without property and all women were excluded from political rights. Only for a brief period under the Jacobins did all adult males enjoy suffrage. However, the Napoleonic Code went back to limited suffrage and reduced women to the status of a minor, subject to the authority of fathers and husbands. Throughout the nineteenth and early twentieth centuries women and non-propertied men organised opposition movements demanding equal political rights.

Answer the following MCQs by choosing the most appropriate option

9.1 Ideas of national unity in early-nineteenth-century Europe were closely allied to the ideology of:

    (a) Idealism   (b) Conservatism   (c) Socialism   (d) Liberalism

9.2 For the new middle classes liberalism stood for:

    (a) Freedom for the Community   (b) Equality before Law

    (c) both (a) and (b)   (d) only (a)

9.3 In revolutionary France, the right to vote and to get elected was granted exclusively to:

    (a) men only   (b) property-owning men only

    (c) both men and women   (d) all adult citizens

9.4 The Napoleonic Code treated women as to the:

(a)   status of a minor
(b)   subject to the authority of fathers and husbands.

(c)   both (a) and (b)
(d)   none of the above

10.   **Read the text given below and answer the following questions.**

The distribution pattern of the Railway network in the country has been largely influenced by physiographic, economic and administrative factors. The northern plains with their vast level land, high population density and rich agricultural resources provided the most favourable condition for their growth. However, a large number of rivers requiring construction of bridges across their wide beds posed some obstacles. In the hilly terrains of the peninsular region, railway tracts are laid through low hills, gaps or tunnels. The Himalayan mountainous regions too are unfavourable for the construction of railway lines due to high relief, sparse population and lack of economic opportunities. Likewise, it was difficult to lay railway lines on the sandy plain of western Rajasthan, swamps of Gujarat, forested tracks of Madhya Pradesh, Chhattisgarh, Odisha and Jharkhand. The contiguous stretch of Sahyadri could be crossed only through gaps or passes (Ghats). In recent times, the development of the Konkan railway along the west coast has facilitated the movement of passengers and goods in this most important economic region of India. It has also faced a number of problems such as sinking of track in some stretches and landslides.

10.1 Which of the following factors has influenced the distribution pattern of the Railway network in the country?

(a) Legislative
(b) Administrative
(c) Economic
(d) Both (b) and (c)

10.2 Which of the following has been an obstacle in the development of Railways in the Northern Plains?

(a) High population density
(b) Vast agricultural tracts

(c) Large number of rivers
(d) Dense forests

10.3 Which of the following factor make the construction of railway lines unfavourable in the Himalayan region?

(a) High population density
(b) Vast agricultural tracts

(c) Large number of rivers
(d) Lack of economic opportunities

10.4 The contiguous stretch of Sahyadri could be crossed only through:

(a) Airways
(b) Roadways
(c) Bridges
(d) Ghats

11.   **Read the given extract and answer the following questions**

Every party in the country has to register with the Election Commission. While the Commission treats all parties equally, it offers some special facilities to large and established parties. These parties are given a unique symbol – only the official candidates of that party can use that election symbol. Parties that get this privilege and some other special facilities are 'recognised' by the Election Commission for this purpose. That is why these parties are called, 'recognised political parties'. The Election

Commission has laid down detailed criteria of the proportion of votes and seats that a party must get in order to be a recognised party. A party that secures at least six per cent of the total votes in an election to the Legislative Assembly of a State and wins at least two seats is recognised as a State party. A party that secures at least six per cent of the total votes in Lok Sabha elections or Assembly elections in four States and wins at least four seats in the Lok Sabha is recognised as a national party.

11.1 With reference to the Election Commission, which of the following statements is **incorrect**?

(a) It treats all political parties equally

(b) It gives some special facilities to large parties

(c) The symbols allotted to the political parties can be used by any of its members.

(d) Every party in the country has to register with the Election Commission.

11.2 Which of the following factors gives recognition to the political parties?

(a) Cadre Strength   (b) Privilege   (c) Transparency   (d) Popularity

11.3 How many seats in the Lok Sabha elections should a political party win to be recognised as a National Party?

(a) Six   (b) Four   (c) Eight   (d) Five

11.4 What Percent of the total vote in an assembly election should a political party win to be recognised as a state party?

(a) Six   (b) Four   (c) Eight   (d) Five

12. **Read the source given below and answer the following questions**

The idea of development or progress has always been with us. We have aspirations or desires about what we would like to do and how we would like to live. Similarly, we have ideas about what a country should be like. What are the essential things that we require? Can life be better for all? How should people live together? Can there be more equality? Development involves thinking about these questions and about the ways in which we can work towards achieving these goals. This is because the way we live today is influenced by the past. We can't desire for change without being aware of this. In the same way, it is only through a democratic political process that these hopes and possibilities can be achieved in real life.

12.1 According to the passage, the idea of development:

(a) is completely novel to us   (b) has never been there before 20th century

(c) has always been with us   (d) is different from progress

12.2 Development involves thinking about:

(a) Equality   (b) Way of life   (c) Nature of country   (d) all of the above

12.3 The way we live today is influenced by the

(a) Present state   (b) Past   (c) Future dreams   (d) God

12.4 Only through a the hopes and possibilities can be achieved in real life:

    (a) Monarchy and absolutism   (b) Authority and repression

    (c) Liberty and equality   (d) Democratic political process

13.   **Read the source given below and answer the questions that follows**

In February 1922 Mahatma Gandhi decided to withdraw the Non-cooperation Movement. He felt the movement was turning violent in many places and Satyagrahis needed to be properly trained before they would be ready for mass struggles. Within the Congress. some leader were by now tired of mass struggles and wanted to participate in elections to the Provincial Councils that had been set up by the Government of India Act of 1919. They felt that it was important to oppose British policies within the councils, argue for reform and also demonstrate that these councils were not truly democratic. CR Das and Motilal Nehru formed the Swaraj Party within the congress to argue for a return to council politics. But younger leader like Jawaharlal Nehru and Subhas Chandra Bose pressed for more redical mass agitation and for full independence. In such a situation of internal debate and dissension two factors again shaped Indian politics towards the late 1920s. The first was the effect of the worldwide economic depression. Agricultural prices began to fall from 1926 and collapsed after 1930. As the demand for agricultural goods fell and exports declined, peasants found it difficult to sell their harvest and pay their revenue. By 1930, the countryside was in turmoil.

Against this background the new Tory Government in Britain constituted a Statutory Commission under Sir John Simon. Set up in response to the Nationalist Movement, the commission was to look into the functioning off the Constitutional System in India and suggest changes. The problem was that the commission did not have a single Indian member. They were all British.

Answer the following MCQs by choosing the most appropriate option

13.1. Identify the reason behind the withdrawal of the Non-Cooperation Movement by Gandhiji.

    (a) Movement became violent.

    (b) Satyagrahis needed to be properly trained.

    (c) people took it lightly

    (d) Both (a) and (b)

13.2 Which of the following statements correctly describes the formation of the Swaraj Party?

    (a) Leaders were tired of mass struggle.

    (b) Leaders wanted more power.

    (c) Leaders wanted to participate in the elections of Provincial Councils.

    (d) Both (a) and (c)

13.3. What were the two important factors that influenced Indian politics during the late 1920?

    (a) The effect of worldwide economic depression.

    (b) Countryside was in turmoil as the peasants found it difficult to sell their harvests and pay the revenue.

    (c) The British government tried to establish the supremacy on export.

    (d) Both (a) and (b)

13.4 By 1930, Tory government in Britain constituted a Statutory Commission under Sir John Simon whose work was to

    (a) look into the functioning of the Constitutional System in India.

    (b) suggest required changes

    (c) ignore the voice of India.

    (d) All of the above

14.   **Read the source given below and answer the questions that follows**

In the early years, the cotton textile industry was concentrated in the cotton growing belt of Maharashtra and Gujarat. Availability of raw cotton, market, transport including accessible port facilities, labour, moist climate, etc. contributed towards its localisation. This industry has close links with agriculture and provides a living to formers, cotton ball puckers and worker engaged in ginning spinning, weaving, dyeing, designing, packaging, tailoring and sewing. The industry by creating demands supports many other industries, such as chemicals and dyes, packaging materials and engineering works.

While spinning continues to be centralised in Maharashtra, Gujarat and Tamil Nadu, weaving is highly decentralised to provide scope for incorporating traditional skill and designs of weaving in cotton, silk, zari, embroidery etc. India has world class production in spinning, but weaving supplies low quality of fabric as it cannot use much of the high quality yarn produced in the country. Weaving in done by handloom powerloom and mills.

The hundspun khadi provides large scale employments to weavers in their homes as a cottage industry. India exports yarn to Japan. Other importers of cotton goods from India are USA, UK Russia. France, East European countries, Nepal, Singapore, Sri Lanka and African countries.

Answer the following MCQs by choosing the most appropriate option

14.1 The source given above relates to which of the following options?

    (a) Jute textile industry   (b) Cotton textile industry

    (c) Silk textile industry   (d) Woollen textile industry

14.2 In the early years, the cotton textile industry was concentrated in the cotton growing belt of _______ and ______.

    (a) West Bengal, Assam   (b) Maharashtra, Bihar

    (c) Rajasthan, Gujarat   (d) Maharashtra Gujarat

14.3. Which off the following industries is not related with ginning, spinning, weaving, dyeing tailoring, etc?

    (a) Sugar industry   (b) Cotton textile industry

    (c) Woollen industry   (d) Jute industry

14.4. India exports its yarn to which of the following countries?

    (a) UK   (b) Russia

    (c) france   (d) All of the above

15.   **Read the source and answer the following questions that follow.**

No society can fully and permanently resolve conflicts among different groups. But we can certainly learn to respect these differences and we can also evolve mechanisms to negotiate the differences. Democracy is best suited to produce this outcome. Non-democratic regimes often turn a blind eye to or suppress internal social differences. Ability to handle social differences, divisions and conflicts is thus a definite plus point of democratic regimes. But the example of Sri Lanka reminds us that a democracy must fulfill two conditions in order to achieve this outcome:

- It is necessary to understand that democracy is not simply rule by majority option. The majority always needs to work with the minority so that governments function to represent the general view. Majority and minority option are not permanent.

- It is also necessary that rule by majority does not become rule by majority community in terms of religion or race or linguistic group, etc. Rule by majority means that in case of every decision or in case of every election, different persons and groups may and can form a majority. Democracy remains democracy only as long as every citizen has a chance of being in majority at some point of time. If someone is barred from being in majority on the basis of birth, then the democratic rule ceases to be accommodative for that person or group.

Answer the following MCQs by choosing the most appropriate option

15.1. The conflicts among different groups can be resolved in the best way through __________

    (a) Democracy   (b) Dictatorship

    (c) Monarchical system   (d) None of the above

15.2. The plus point of democratic regimes is __________

    (a) ability to handle social differences   (b) divisions and conflicts are resolved

    (c) economic development   (d) Both (a) and (b)

15.3. Democracy always needs to work with the __________ so that governments function torepresent the general view.

    (a) majority   (b) minority

    (c) All the members of the parliament   (d) Members of both the Houses

15.4. Rule by majority does not become rule by majority community in terms of

    (a) Religion   (b) Race

    (c) Linguistic Groups   (d) All of the above

16. **Read the source and answer the following questions that follows**

In general, MNCs set up production where it is close to the markets; where there is skilled and unskilled labour available at low costs; and where the availability of other factors of production is assured. In addition, MNCs might look for government policies that look after their interests. You will read more about the policies later in the chapter.

Having assured themselves of these conditions, MNCs set up factories and offices for production. The money that is spent to buy assets such as land, building, machines and other equipment is called investment. Investment made by MNCs is called foreign investment. Any investment is made with the hope that these assets will earn profits.

At times MNCs set up production jointly with some of the local companies of the countries. The benefit to the local company of such joint production is two-fold. First, MNCs can provide money for additional investments, like buying new machines fro faster production. Second MNCs might bring with them the latest technology for production. But the most common route for MNCs might bright with them the latest technology for production. But the most common route for MNC investments is to buy up local companies and then to expand production. MNCs with huge wealth can quite easily do so. To take an example, Cargill Foods, a very large American MNC, has brought over smaller INdian companies such as Parakh Foods has built a large marketing network in various parts of India, where its brand was well-reputed. Also Parakh Foods had four oil refineries, whose control has now shifted to Cargill. is now the largest producer o edible oil in India, with a capacity to make 5 million pouches daily.

Answer the following MCQs by choosing the most appropriate option

16.1 The source given above relates to which of the following options?

    (a) MNCs   (b) Demand deposits

    (c) International competition   (d) Foreign collaboration

16.2. According to the above passage, which condition is required to set up a factory by an MNC in a country?

    (a) Closeness of market   (b) Availability of skilled and unskilled labour.

    (c) Favourable government policies   (d) All of the above

16.3. The money that is spent to buy assets such as land, building, machines and equipment is known as

    (a) cost of production   (b) investment

    (c) cost of final goods and services   (d) None of the above

16.4. The largest producer of edible oil in India is

    (a) Paras   (b) Parakh Foods

    (c) Corgill Foods   (d) None of the above

17. **Read the source given below and answer the questions that follows:**

The silk routes are a good example of vibrant pre-modern trade and cultural links between distant parts of the world. The name 'silk routes' points to the importance of West-bound Chinese silk cargoes along this route. Historians have identified several silk routes, over land and by sea, knitting together vast regions of Asia, and linking Asia with Europe and northern Africa. They are known to have existed since before the Christian era and thrived almost till the fifteenth century. But Chinese pottery also travelled the same route, as did textiles and spices from India and Southeast Asia. In return, precious metals – gold and silver – flowed from Europe to Asia. Trade and cultural exchange always went hand in hand. Early Christian missionaries almost certainly travelled this route to Asia, as did early Muslim preachers a few centuries later. Much before all this, Buddhism emerged from eastern India and spread in several directions through intersecting points on the silk routes.

Answer the following MCQs by choosing the most appropriate option

17.1 The silk routes are a good example of:

  (a) Post-modern trade   (b) Cultural links

  (c) both (a) and (b)   (d) None of the above

17.2 The name 'silk routes' points to the importance of West-bound_____________ cargoes along this route.

  (a) Post-modern trade   (b) Cultural links

  (c) Chinese silk   (d) Western Silk

17.3 With reference to the ancient silk route, consider the following statements:

1. The silk routes passed through land only

2. It linked Asia with Europe and North Africa

Which of the statement(s) given above is/are correct?

  (a) 1 only   (b) 2 only   (c) Both 1 and 2   (d) Neither 1 nor 2

17.4 The preachers of which of the following religions used the silk route to spread their ideas?

  (a) Islam   (b) Buddhism   (c) Christianity   (d) All of the above

18. **Read the text given below and answer the following questions**

Planning is the widely accepted strategy for judicious use of resources. It has importance in a country like India, which has enormous diversity in the availability of resources. There are regions which are rich in certain types of resources but are deficient in some other resources. There are some regions which can be considered self sufficient in terms of the availability of resources and there are some regions which have acute shortage of some vital resources. For example, the states of Jharkhand, Chhattisgarh and Madhya Pradesh are rich in minerals and coal deposits. Arunachal Pradesh has abundance of water resources but lacks in infrastructural development. The state of Rajasthan is very well endowed with solar and wind energy but lacks in water resources. The cold desert of Ladakh is relatively isolated from the rest of the country. It has very rich cultural heritage but it is deficient in water, infrastructure and some vital minerals. This calls for balanced resource planning at the national, state, regional and local levels.

Answer the following MCQs by choosing the most appropriate option.

18.1 Why do you think planning of resources is important to India?

    (a) Because it lacks natural resources

    (b) Due to its concentration in one part of the country

    (c) It has enormous diversity in the availability of resources

    (d) None of the above

18.2 Which of the following statement(s) is/are correct?

    (a) Judicious planning of natural resources is important

    (b) There are regions which are rich in certain types of resources but are deficient in some other resources.

    (c) India has enormous diversity in the availability of resources

    (d) All of the above

18.3 Arunachal Pradesh has abundance of resources but lacks in infrastructural development.

    (a) Coal   (b) Human   (c) Cattle   (d) Water

18.4 With reference to the region of Ladakh, consider the following statements:

    1. It is well integrated with rest of the country.

    2. It has abundant water resources.

    Which of the statement(s) given above is/are correct?

    (a) 1 only   (b) 2 only   (c) Both 1 and 2   (d) Neither 1 nor 2

19. Read the given extract and answer the following questions

Political parties are easily one of the most visible institutions in a democracy. For most ordinary citizens, democracy is equal to political parties. If you travel to remote parts of our country and speak to the less educated citizens, you could come across people who may not know anything about our Constitution or about the nature of our government. But chances are that they would know something about our political parties. At the same time this visibility does not mean popularity. Most people tend to be very critical of political parties. They tend to blame parties for all that is wrong with our democracy and our political life. Parties have become identified with social and political divisions. Therefore, it is natural to ask – do we need political parties at all? About hundred years ago there were few countries of the world that had any political party. Now there are few that do not have parties. Why did political parties become so omnipresent in democracies all over the world?

Answer the following MCQs by choosing the most appropriate option

19.1 For most ordinary citizens, _______ is equal to political parties.

   (a) Organisation   (b) Election   (c) Democracy   (d) Party Workers

19.2 Consider the following statements:

   1.   Most citizens know about constitution, just like they know about political parties

   2.   Political parties are easily visible institutions.

   Which of the statement(s) given above is/are correct?

   (a) 1 only   (b) 2 only   (c) Both 1 and 2   (d) Neither 1 nor 2

19.3 Consider the following statements:

   1. More visibility means the better popularity of political parties among citizens

   2. Most people tend to be very critical of political parties

   Which of the statement(s) given above is/are correct?

   (a) 1 only   (b) 2 only   (c) Both 1 and 2   (d) Neither 1 nor 2

19.4 Parties have become identified with social and _______ divisions.

   (a) Economic   (b) Ideological   (c) Caste   (d) Political

20.   **Read the source given below and answer the following questions.**

As consumers in today's world, some of us have a wide choice of goods and services before us. The latest models of digital cameras, mobile phones and televisions made by the leading manufacturers of the world are within our reach. Every season, new models of automobiles can be seen on Indian roads. Gone are the days when Ambassador and Fiat were the only cars on Indian roads. Today, Indians are buying cars produced by nearly all the top companies in the world. A similar explosion of brands can be seen for many other goods: from shirts to televisions to processed fruit juices. Such wide-ranging choice of goods in our markets is a relatively recent phenomenon. You wouldn't have found such a wide variety of goods in Indian markets even two decades back. In a matter of years, our markets have been transformed. Until the middle of the twentieth century, production was largely organised within countries. What crossed the boundaries of these countries were raw materials, food stuff and finished products. Colonies such as India exported raw materials and food stuff and imported finished goods. Trade was the main channel connecting distant countries.

Answer the following MCQs by choosing the most appropriate option

20.1 As consumers in today's world, some of us have a _______ of goods and services before us.

   (a) Limited choice   (b) Wide choice

   (c) No choice   (d) None of the above

20.2 Which of the following car's name finds a mention in the passage?

(a) Ambassador   (b) Maruti   (c) Fiat   (d) Both a and c

20.3 Consider the following statements:

1.   An explosion of brands can be seen for goods: from shirts to televisions to processed fruit juices.

2.   Such wide-ranging choice of goods in our markets is not a recent phenomenon.

Which of the statement(s) given above is/are correct?

(a) 1 only   (b) 2 only   (c) Both 1 and 2   (d) Neither 1 nor 2

20.4 Which of the following was the main channel connecting distant countries?

(a) Currency   (b) Literature   (c) Trade   (d) Friendship

21.   **Read the source given below and answer the questions that follows:**

The earliest factories in England came up by the 1730s. But it was only in the late eighteenth century that the number of factories multiplied. The first symbol of the new era was cotton. Its production boomed in the late nineteenth century. In 1760 Britain was importing 2.5 million pounds of raw cotton to feed its cotton industry. By 1787 this import soared to 22 million pounds. This increase was linked to a number of changes within the process of production. Let us look briefly at some of these. A series of inventions in the eighteenth century increased the efficacy of each step of the production process (carding, twisting and spinning, and rolling). They enhanced the output per worker, enabling each worker to produce more, and they made possible the production of stronger threads and yarn. Then Richard Arkwright created the cotton mill. Till this time, as you have seen, cloth production was spread all over the countryside and carried out within village households. But now, the costly new machines could be purchased, set up and maintained in the mill.

Answer the following MCQs by choosing the most appropriate option

21.1 The earliest factories in England came up in the

(a) 17th Century   (b) 16th Century   (c) 18th Century   (d) 19th Century

21.2 What was the first symbol of new era?

(a) Iron and Steel   (b) Indigo   (c) Railways   (d) Cotton

21.3 Consider the following statements:

1.   Cotton production boomed in the late nineteenth century

2.   Britain was the chief exporter of raw cotton in the late nineteenth century

Which of the statement(s) given above is/are correct?

(a) 1 only   (b) 2 only   (c) Both 1 and 2   (d) Neither 1 nor 2

21.4 Who created the cotton mill?

(a) James Mill   (b) Richard Arkwright (c) Richard Heagraves (d) Karl Arkwright

22. **Read the source given below and answer the questions that follows:**

Industrial locations are complex in nature. These are influenced by availability of raw material, labour, capital, power and market, etc. It is rarely possible to find all these factors available at one place. Consequently, manufacturing activity tends to locate at the most appropriate place where all the factors of industrial location are either available or can be arranged at lower cost. After an industrial activity starts, urbanisation follows. Sometimes, industries are located in or near the cities. Thus, industrialisation and urbanisation go hand in hand. Cities provide markets and also provide services such as banking, insurance, transport, labour, consultants and financial advice, etc. to the industry. Many industries tend to come together to make use of the advantages offered by the urban centres known as agglomeration economies. Gradually, a large industrial agglomeration takes place. In the pre-Independence period, most manufacturing units were located in places from the point of view of overseas trade such as Mumbai, Kolkata, Chennai, etc. Consequently, there emerged certain pockets of industrially developed urban centres surrounded by a huge agricultural rural hinterland.

Answer the following MCQs by choosing the most appropriate option

22.1 Which of the following factors influence the location of industry?

    1.   Availability of raw material   2. Labour   3. Capital,

    4.   Government   5. Market

   Choose the correct answer using the codes given below:

   (a) 1, 2, 3 and 4   (b) 1, 2, and 5 only   (c) 1, 3, 4 and 5 only (d) 1, 2, 3 and 5 only

22.2 After an industrial activity starts, _______________ follows.

   (a) Colonisation   (b) Industrialisation   (c) Exploitation   (d) Urbanisation

22.3 Which of the following services are provided by the cities to the industry?

   (a) Banking   (b) Consultation   (c) Transportation   (d) All of the above

22.4 Consider the following statements:

    1.   Many industries come together to make use of the advantages offered by the urban centres known as agglomeration economies.

    2.   In the pre-Independence period, most manufacturing units were located near agricultural rural hinterland.

   Which of the statement(s) given above is/are correct?

   (a) 1 only   (b) 2 only   (c) Both 1 and 2   (d) Neither 1 nor 2

23. **Read the given extract and answer the following questions.**

Perhaps more than development, it is reasonable to expect democracies to reduce economic disparities. Even when a country achieves economic growth, will wealth be distributed in such a way that all citizens of the country will have a share and lead a better life? Is economic growth in democracies accompanied by increased inequalities among the people? Or do democracies lead to a just distribution of goods and opportunities? Democracies are based on political equality. All individuals have equal weight in electing representatives. Parallel to the process of bringing individuals into the political arena on an equal footing, we find growing economic inequalities. A small number of ultra-rich enjoy a highly disproportionate share of wealth and incomes. Not only that, their share in the total income of the country has been increasing. Those at the bottom of the society have very little to depend upon. Their incomes have been declining. Sometimes they find it difficult to meet their basic needs of life, such as food, clothing, house, education and health.

Answer the following MCQs by choosing the most appropriate option

23.1 More than development, it is reasonable to expect democracies to reduce which disparity?

    (a) Social   (b) Political   (c) Developmental   (d) Economic

23.2 Consider the following statements:

    1.   Democracies are based on political equality.

    2.   All individuals have equal weight in electing representatives.

Which of the statements given above is/are correct?

    (a) 1 only   (b) 2 only   (c) Both 1 and 2   (d) Neither 1 nor 2

23.3 Who enjoys a highly disproportionate share of wealth and incomes?

    (a) Ultra-rich   (b) Middle class

    (c) Upper caste   (d) People at bottom of the society

23.4 Which of the following according to the passage is/are basic need of life?

    (a) Food   (b) Clothing   (c) Education   (d) All of the above

24. **Read the source given below and answer the following questions.**

Every loan agreement specifies an interest rate which the borrower must pay to the lender along with the repayment of the principal. In addition, lenders may demand collateral (security) against loans. Collateral is an asset that the borrower owns (such as land, building, vehicle, livestocks, deposits with banks) and uses this as a guarantee to a lender until the loan is repaid. If the borrower fails to repay the loan, the lender has the right to sell the asset or collateral to obtain payment. Property such as land titles, deposits with banks, livestock are some common examples of collateral used for borrowing. Interest rate, collateral and documentation requirement, and the mode of repayment together comprise what is called the terms of credit. The terms of credit vary substantially from one credit arrangement to another. They may vary depending on the nature of the lender and the borrower.

Answer the following MCQs by choosing the most appropriate option

24.1 Every loan agreement specifies a/an _______________ which the borrower must pay along with the repayment of the principal.

    (a) Investment rate   (b) Interest rate   (c) Collateral   (d) Time

24.2 Which of the following is/are example(s) of collateral?

(a) Deposit with a bank   (b) Livestock   (c) Family members   (d) Both a and b

24.3 Which of the following is/are included in the terms of credit?

(a) Collateral   (b) Interest rate   (c) Time duration   (d) All of the above

24.4 Consider the following statements:

1. The terms of credit vary substantially from one credit arrangement to another.

2. The terms of credit may vary depending on the nature of the lender and the borrower.

Which of the statements given above is/are correct?

(a) 1 only   (b) 2 only   (c) Both 1 and 2   (d) Neither 1 nor 2

25. **Read the source given below and answer the questions that follows:**

Emboldened with his success, Gandhiji in 1919 decided to launch a nationwide satyagraha against the proposed Rowlatt Act (1919). This Act had been hurriedly passed through the Imperial Legislative Council despite the united opposition of the Indian members. It gave the government enormous powers to repress political activities, and allowed detention of political prisoners without trial for two years. Mahatma Gandhi wanted non-violent civil disobedience against such unjust laws, which would start with a hartal on 6 April. Rallies were organised in various cities, workers went on strike in railway workshops, and shops closed down. Alarmed by the popular upsurge, and scared that lines of communication such as the railways and telegraph would be disrupted, the British administration decided to clamp down on nationalists. Local leaders were picked up from Amritsar, and Mahatma Gandhi was barred from entering Delhi. On 10 April, the police in Amritsar fired upon a peaceful procession, provoking widespread attacks on banks, post offices and railway stations. Martial law was imposed and General Dyer took command.

Answer the following MCQs by Choosing the most appropriate option

25.1 In 1919 Gandhiji decided to launch a nationwide satyagraha against

(a) Partition of Bengal   (b) Salt Tax

(c) Foreign Cloths   (d) Rowlatt Act

25.2 The opinion of Indian members of the Imperial Legislative Council was

(a) Divided   (b) Inconclusive

(c) United   (d) Neutral

25.3 Alarmed by the popular upsurge the British administration decided to

(a) Support the protestors   (b) Cancelled the Act

(c) Suspend the governor   (d) clamp down on nationalist

25.4 Mahatma Gandhi was barred to enter which of the following place?

    (a) Delhi
    (b) Amritsar

    (c) Kolkata
    (d) Champaran

26.   Read the text given below and answer the following questions.

Soil is the most important renewable natural resource. It is the medium of plant growth and supports different types of living organisms on the earth. The soil is a living system. It takes millions of years to form soil upto a few cm in depth. Relief, parent rock or bed rock, climate, vegetation and other forms of life and time are important factors in the formation of soil. Various forces of nature such as change in temperature, actions of running water, wind and glaciers, activities of decomposers etc. contribute to the formation of soil. Chemical and organic changes which take place in the soil are equally important. Soil also consists of organic (humus) and inorganic materials. On the basis of the factors responsible for soil formation, colour, thickness, texture, age, chemical and physical properties, the soils of India can be classified in different types. Alluvial soil is the most widely spread and important soil. In fact, the entire northern plains are made of alluvial soil. These have been deposited by three important Himalayan river systems– the Indus, the Ganga and the Brahmaputra. These soils also extend in Rajasthan and Gujarat through a narrow corridor. Alluvial soil is also found in the eastern coastal plains particularly in the deltas of the Mahanadi, the Godavari, the Krishna and the Kaveri rivers.

Answer the following MCQs by choosing the most appropriate option

26.1. With reference to soil, Consider the following statements:

    1.   It is the most important renewable natural resource

    2.   The soil is a non-living system.

Which of the statement(s) given above is/are correct?

    (a) 1 only
    (b) 2 only

    (c) Both 1 and 2
    (d) Neither 1 nor 2

26.2 Which of the following factors affect the formation of soil?

    (a) Parent rock
    (b) Climate

    (c) Biological activity
    (d) All of the above

26.3 In India, almost the entire northern plains are made of:

    (a) Regur Soil
    (b) Laterite soil

    (c) Alluvial Soil
    (d) Red Soil

26.4 Which of the following rivers does not deposit alluvial soil in the northern plains?

    (a) Kaveri
    (b) Krishna

    (c) Godavari
    (d) All of the above

27. Read the given extract and answer the following questions.

Power can be shared among governments at different levels – a general government for the entire country and governments at the provincial or regional level. Such a general government for the entire country is usually called federal government. In India, we refer to it as the Central or Union Government. The governments at the provincial or regional level are called by different names in different countries. In India, we call them State Governments. This system is not followed in all countries. There are many countries where there are no provincial or state governments. But in those countries like ours, where there are different levels of government, the constitution clearly lays down the powers of different levels of government. This is what they did in Belgium, but was refused in Sri Lanka. This is called federal division of power. The same principle can be extended to levels of government lower than the State government, such as the municipality and panchayat. Let us call division of powers involving higher and lower levels of government vertical division of power.

Answer the following MCQs by Choosing the most appropriate option

27.1 The general government for the entire country is usually called

    (a) Parliament

    (b) Local Government

    (c) Provincial Government

    (d) Federal Government

27.2 In India, the federal government is also known as

    (a) Central Government

    (b) Panchayati Raj

    (c) Union Government

    (d) Both a and c

27.3 Consider the following statements:

    1. The system of provincial governments is not followed in all countries.

    2. In India, the regional governments are called Panchayats.

Which of the statement(s) given above is/are correct?

    (a) 1 only

    (b) 2 only

    (c) Both 1 and 2

    (d) Neither 1 nor 2

27.4 The division of powers involving higher and lower levels of government is________ division of power.

    (a) Parallel

    (b) Vertical

    (c) Horizontal

    (d) Equal

28. Read the source given below and answer the following questions-

In the last twenty years, globalisation of the Indian economy has come a long way. Globalisation and greater competition among producers - both local and foreign producers - has been of advantage to consumers, particularly the well-off sections in the urban areas. There is greater choice before these consumers who now enjoy improved quality and lower prices for several products. As a result, these people today, enjoy much higher standards of living than was possible earlier. Among producers and workers, the impact of globalisation has not been uniform. Firstly, MNCs have increased their investments in India over the past 20 years, which means investing in India has been beneficial for them. MNCs have been interested in industries such as cell phones, automobiles, electronics, soft drinks, fast food or services such as banking in urban areas. These products have a large number of well-off buyers. In these industries and services, new jobs have been created. Also, local companies supplying raw materials, etc. to these industries have prospered. Secondly, several of the top Indian companies have been able to benefit from the increased competition. They have invested in newer technology and production methods and raised their production standards. Some have gained from successful

Answer the following MCQs by Choosing the most appropriate option

28.1 Which of the following has been of advantage to consumers?

(a) Competition
(b) Globalisation

(c) Both a and b
(d) None of the above

28.2 Among producers and _________ the impact of globalisation have not been uniform.

(a) Buyers
(b) Farmers

(c) Suppliers
(d) Workers

28.3 MNCs have been interested in industries such as:

(a) Cell-phone
(b) soft drinks

(c) fast food
(d) all of the above

28.4 Consider the following statements:

1.   Several top Indian companies have been in loss from the increased competition.

2.   Investments in newer technology and production methods have raised the production standards

Which of the statement(s) given above is/are correct?

(a) 1 only
(b) 2 only

(c) Both 1 and 2
(d) Neither 1 nor 2

29.   **Read the source given below and answer the questions that follows:**

The example of indentured labour migration from India illustrates the two-sided nature of the nineteenth-century world. It was a world of faster economic growth as well as great misery, higher incomes for some and poverty for others, technological advances in some areas and new forms of coercion in others. In the nineteenth century, hundreds of thousands of Indian and Chinese labourers went to work on plantations, in mines, and in road and railway construction projects around the world. In India, indentured labourers were hired under contracts which promised return travel to India after they had worked five years on their employer's plantation. Most Indian indentured workers came from the present-day regions of eastern Uttar Pradesh, Bihar, central India and the dry districts of Tamil Nadu.

In the mid-nineteenth century these regions experienced many changes – cottage industries declined, land rents rose, lands were cleared for mines and plantations. All this affected the lives of the poor: they failed to pay their rents, became deeply indebted and were forced to migrate in search of work.

Answer the following MCQs by choosing the most appropriate option

29.1 Which of the following is/are included in the two-sided nature of the nineteenth-century world?

    (a) great misery   (b)   faster economic growth

    (c) technological advances   (d)   All of the above

29.2 Return travel to India after how many years of work was offered to the indentured labourers?

    (a) 3   (b) 5   (c) 7   (d) 10

29.3 Most Indian indentured workers came from the present-day regions of:

    (a) Uttar Pradesh   (b)   Bihar

    (c) Tamil Nadu   (d)   All of the above

29.4 Consider the following statements:

    1.   In the mid-eighteenth century cottage industries declined.

    2.   Chinese labourers went to work on plantations, in mines, and in road and railway construction projects around the world.

    Which of the statement(s) given above is/are correct?

    (a) 1 only   (b)   2 only

    (c) Both 1 and 2   (d)   Neither 1 nor 2

30. **Read the text given below and answer the following questions.**

Various types of food and fibre crops, vegetables and fruits, spices and condiments, etc. constitute some of the important crops grown in the country. India has three cropping seasons — rabi, kharif and zaid. Rabi crops are sown in winter from October to December and harvested in summer from April to June. Some of the important rabi crops are wheat, barley, peas, gram and mustard. Though, these crops are grown in large parts of India, states from the north and northwestern parts such as Punjab, Haryana, Himachal Pradesh, Jammu and Kashmir, Uttarakhand and Uttar Pradesh are important for the production of wheat and other rabi crops. Availability of precipitation during winter months due to the western temperate cyclones helps in the success of these crops. However, the success of the green revolution in Punjab, Haryana, western Uttar Pradesh and parts of Rajasthan has also been an important factor in the growth of the abovementioned rabi crops. Kharif crops are grown with the onset of monsoon in different parts of the country and these are harvested in September-October. Important crops grown during this season are paddy, maize, jowar, bajra, tur (arhar), moong, urad, cotton, jute, groundnut and soyabean. Some of the most important rice-growing regions are Assam, West Bengal, coastal regions of Odisha, Andhra Pradesh, Telangana, Tamil Nadu, Kerala and Maharashtra, particularly the (Konkan coast) along with Uttar Pradesh and Bihar. Recently, paddy has also become an important crop of Punjab and Haryana. In states like Assam, West Bengal and Odisha, three crops of paddy are grown in a year. These are Aus, Aman and Boro. In between the rabi and the kharif seasons, there is a short season during the summer months known as the Zaid season.

Answer the following MCQs by choosing the most appropriate option

30.1 How many cropping seasons does India have?

(a) 1　　　　　　(b) 2　　　　　　(c) 3　　　　　　(d) 4

30.2 Which of the following is not a rabi crop?

(a) Barley　　　　(b) Mustard　　　　(c) Rice　　　　(d) Peas

30.3 Availability of precipitation during winter months due to the western temperate cyclones helps in the success of which crops?

(a) Rabi　　　　(b) Zaid　　　　(c) Kharif　　　　(d) All of the above

30.4 In states like Assam, West Bengal and Odisha, three crops of _______ are grown in a year.

(a) Paddy　　　　(b) Wheat　　　　(c) Gram　　　　(d) All of the above

31.　**Read the given extract and answer the following questions.**

The exact balance of power between the central and the state government varies from one federation to another. This balance depends mainly on the historical context in which the federation was formed. There are two kinds of routes through which federations have been formed. The first route involves independent States coming together on their own to form a bigger unit, so that by pooling sovereignty and retaining identity they can increase their security. This type of 'coming together' federations include the USA, Switzerland and Australia. In this first category of federations, all the constituent States usually have equal power and are strong vis-à-vis the federal government. The second route is where a large country decides to divide its power between the constituent States and the national government. India, Spain and Belgium are examples of this kind of 'holding together' federations. In this second category, the central government tends to be more powerful vis-à-vis the States. Very often different constituent units of the federation have unequal powers. Some units are granted special powers.

Answer the following MCQs by choosing the most appropriate option

31.1 The exact balance of power between the central and the state government

(a) Remains same for every federation　　　　　(b) Varies between one federation to another

(c) Can never be achieved　　　　　(d) is given by the supreme court

31.2 When independent States come together on their own to form a bigger unit

(a) They lose their identity　　　　　(b) They compromise with their security

(c) They pool their sovereignty　　　　　(d) All of the above

31.3 Which of the following country is not an example of coming together federation?

   (a) USA   (b) Switzerland

   (c) India   (d) Australia

31.4 In case of holding together federation:

   (a) Center is more powerful   (b) States are more powerful

   (c) Both center and states have equal powers   (d) Panchayats are most powerful

32. **Read the source given below and answer the following questions-**

The organised sector offers jobs that are the most sought-after. But the employment opportunities in the organised sector have been expanding very slowly. It is also common to find many organised sector enterprises in the unorganised sector. They adopt such strategies to evade taxes and refuse to follow laws that protect labourers. As a result, a large number of workers are forced to enter the unorganised sector jobs, which pay a very low salary. They are often exploited and not paid a fair wage. Their earnings are low and not regular. These jobs are not secure and have no other benefits. Since the 1990s, it is also common to see a large number of workers losing their jobs in the organised sector. These workers are forced to take up jobs in the unorganised sector with low earnings. Hence, besides the need for more work, there is also a need for protection and support of the workers in the unorganised sector. Who are these vulnerable people who need protection? In the rural areas, the unorganised sector mostly comprises of landless agricultural labourers, small and marginal farmers, sharecroppers and artisans (such as weavers, blacksmiths, carpenters and goldsmiths). Nearly 80 per cent of rural households in India are in small and marginal farmer category. These farmers need to be supported through adequate facility for timely delivery of seeds, agricultural inputs, credit, storage facilities and marketing outlets.

Answer the following MCQs by choosing the most appropriate option

32.1 Why do we find some organised sector enterprises in the unorganised sector?

   (a) To evade taxes   (b) To avoid following laws

   (c) both a and b   (d) None of the above

32.2 Which of the following is/are not true for the unorganised sector enterprises?

   (a) They exploit workers   (b) They offer better salary

   (c) They give job security   (d) Both b and c

32.3 Which of the following is not an artisan's category?

   (a) Blacksmiths   (b) Carpenters

   (c) Goldsmiths   (d) sharecroppers

32.4 The approximate per cent of rural households in India in small and marginal farmer category is:

   (a) 50   (b) 60   (c) 70   (d) 80

33. **Read the source given below and answer the questions that follows:**

Despite years of stable and rapid growth, not all was well in this post-war world. From the 1960s the rising costs of its overseas involvements weakened the US's finances and competitive strength. The US dollar now no longer commanded confidence as the world's principal currency. It could not maintain its value in relation to gold. This eventually led to the collapse of the system of fixed exchange rates and the introduction of a system of floating exchange rates. From the mid-1970s the international financial system also changed in important ways. Earlier, developing countries could turn to international institutions for loans and development assistance. But now they were forced to borrow from Western commercial banks and private lending institutions. This led to periodic debt crises in the developing world, and lower incomes and increased poverty, especially in Africa and Latin America. The industrial world was also hit by unemployment that began rising from the mid-1970s and remained high until the early 1990s. From the late 1970s MNCs also began to shift production operations to low-wage Asian countries.

Answer the following MCQs by choosing the most appropriate option

33.1 The US dollar no longer commanded confidence as the world's principal currency in the latter half of

(a) 17th Century   (b) 18th Century   (c) 19th Century   (d) 20th Century

33.2 The introduction of a system of floating exchange rates was due to

(a)   Change in dollar-gold relations   (b)   Collapse of fixed exchange rate system

(c)   Involvement of USA overseas   (d)   All of the above

33.3 The periodic debt crises in the developing world included which of the following region/regions

(a)   Latin America   (b)   Western Europe(c)   Africa   (d)   Both a and c

33.4 From the late 1970s MNCs began to shift production operations to low________ wage countries.

(a)   American   (b)   Western European (c)   Asian   (d)   None of the above

34. **Read the test given below and answer the following questions.**

India's food security policy has a primary objective to ensure availability of foodgrains to the common people at an affordable price. It has enabled the poor to have access to food. The focus of the policy is on growth in agriculture production and on fixing the support price for procurement of wheat and rice, to maintain their stocks. Food Corporation of India (FCI) is responsible for procuring and stocking foodgrains, whereas distribution is ensured by public distribution system (PDS). The FCI procures foodgrains from the farmers at the government announced minimum support price (MSP). The government used to provide subsidies on agriculture inputs such as fertilizers, power and water. These subsidies have now reached unsustainable levels and have also led to large scale inefficiencies in the use of these scarce inputs. Excessive and imprudent use of fertilizers and water has led to waterlogging, salinity and depletion of essential micronutrients in the soil. The high MSP, subsidies in input and committed FCI purchases have distorted the cropping pattern. Wheat and paddy crops are being grown more for the MSP they get. Punjab and Haryana are foremost examples. This has also created a serious imbalance in inter-crop parities.

Answer the following MCQs by choosing the most appropriate option

34.1 India's food security policy has a primary objective to ensure availability of foodgrains to the common people at __________ .

  (a) Minimum Support Price   (b) Affordable price

  (c) Cost Price   (d) Lowest price

34.2 In relation to Indian food security policy, the term PDS stand for:

  (a) Price Distribution System   (b) Public Demand System

  (c) People Distribution Scheme   (d) Public Distribution System

34.3 Excessive and imprudent use of fertilizers and water has led to

  (a) Waterlogging and   (b) Salinity

  (c) Depletion of essential micronutrients   (d) All of the above

34.4 The high MSP, subsidies in input and committed FCI purchases have ________ the cropping pattern.

  (a) Distorted   (b) Balanced   (c) Declined   (d) Stopped

35. **Read the given extract and answer the following questions:**

Democracy stands much superior to any other form of government in promoting dignity and freedom of the individual. Every individual wants to receive respect from fellow beings. Often conflicts arise among individuals because some feel that they are not treated with due respect. The passion for respect and freedom are the basis of democracy. Democracies throughout the world have recognised this, at least in principle. This has been achieved in various degrees in various democracies. For societies which have been built for long on the basis of subordination and domination, it is not a simple matter to recognize that all individuals are equal. Take the case of dignity of women. Most societies across the world were historically male dominated societies. Long struggles by women have created some sensitivity today that respect to and equal treatment of women are necessary ingredients of a democratic society. That does not mean that women are actually always treated with respect. But once the principle is recognised, it becomes easier for women to wage a struggle against what is now unacceptable legally and morally. In a non-democratic set up, this unacceptability would not have legal basis because the principle of individual freedom and dignity would not have the legal and moral force there. The same is true of caste inequalities. Democracy in India has strengthened the claims of the disadvantaged and discriminated castes for equal status and equal opportunity. There are instances still of caste-based inequalities and atrocities, but these lack the moral and legal foundations. Perhaps it is the recognition that makes ordinary citizens value their democratic rights.

Answer the following MCQs by choosing the most appropriate option

35.1 The passion for __________ and freedom are the basis of democracy.

(a) Equality   (b) Respect   (c) Liberty (d)   Dignity

35.2 Most societies across the world were historically

(a) Male dominated   (b) Female dominated (c) Female Suppressed   (d)   both a and c

35.3 In India, What according to the passage has strengthened the claims of the disadvantaged and discriminated castes for equal status and equal opportunity?

(a) Democracy   (b) Written constitution   (c) Reservation (d) Discrimination

35.4 Consider the following statements:

1. Across the world women are actually always treated with respect.

2. There are instances still of caste-based inequalities and atrocities, but these lack the moral and legal foundations.

Which of the statements given above is/are correct?

(a) 1 only   (b) 2 only   (c) Both 1 and 2   (d)   Neither 1 nor 2

36. **Read the source given below and answer the questions that follows:**

In recent years, people have tried out some newer ways of providing loans to the poor. The idea is to organise rural poor, in particular women, into small Self Help Groups (SHGs) and pool (collect) their savings. A typical SHG has 15-20 members, usually belonging to one neighbourhood, who meet and save regularly. Saving per member varies from Rs 25 to Rs 100 or more, depending on the ability of the people to save. Members can take small loans from the group itself to meet their needs. The group charges interest on these loans but this is still less than what the moneylender charges. After a year or two, if the group is regular in savings, it becomes eligible for availing loan from the bank. Loan is sanctioned in the name of the group and is meant to create self-employment opportunities for the members. For instance, small loans are provided to the members for releasing mortgaged land, for meeting working capital needs (e.g. buying seeds, fertilisers, raw materials like bamboo and cloth), for housing materials, for acquiring assets like sewing machine, handlooms, cattle, etc. Most of the important decisions regarding the savings and loan activities are taken by the group members. The group decides as regards the loans to be granted — the purpose, amount, interest to be charged, repayment schedule etc. Also, it is the group which is responsible for the repayment of the loan. Any case of non-repayment of loan by any one member is followed up seriously by other members in the group. Because of this feature, banks are willing to lend to the poor women when organised in SHGs, even though they have no collateral as such.

Answer the following MCQs by choosing the most appropriate option

36.1 Which of the following statements is not true for Self Help Groups (SHGs)?

  (a) A typical SHG has 15-20 members   (b) The members of a SHG pool their savings

  (c) Minimum saving contribution is Rs.100(d) The members of a SHG meet and save regularly

36.2 consider the following statements:

  1. SHG Members can take small loans from the group itself to meet their needs.

  2. The group charges no interest on these loans.

  Which of the statements given above is/are correct?

  (a) 1 only   (b) 2 only   (c) Both 1 and 2   (d)   Neither 1 nor 2

36.3 After how many years, if the group is regular in savings, a SHG becomes eligible for availing loan from the bank?

  (a) 5 or 6   (b) 1 or 2   (c) 3 or 4   (d)   2 or 3

36.4 consider the following statements:

  1. Loan is sanctioned in the name of the group and is meant to create self-employment opportunities for the members.

  2. Any case of non-repayment of loan by any one member is followed up seriously by other members in the group.

  Which of the statements given above is/are correct?

  (a) 1 only   (b) 2 only   (c) Both 1 and 2   (d)   Neither 1 nor 2

37. **Read the source given below and answer the questions that follows:**

In Victorian Britain there was no shortage of human labour. Poor peasants and vagrants moved to the cities in large numbers in search of jobs, waiting for work. As you will know, when there is plenty of labour, wages are low. So industrialists had no problem of labour shortage or high wage costs. They did not want to introduce machines that got rid of human labour and required large capital investment. In many industries the demand for labour was seasonal. Gas works and breweries were especially busy through the cold months. So they needed more workers to meet their peak demand. Bookbinders and printers, catering to Christmas demand, too needed extra hands before December. At the waterfront, winter was the time that ships were repaired and spruced up. In all such industries where production fluctuated with the season, industrialists usually preferred hand labour, employing workers for the season. A range of products could be produced only with hand labour. Machines were oriented to producing uniforms, standardised goods for a mass market. But the demand in the market was often for goods with intricate designs and specific shapes. In mid-nineteenth-century Britain, for instance, 500 varieties of hammers were produced and 45 kinds of axes. These required human skill, not mechanical technology. In Victorian Britain, the upper classes – the aristocrats and the bourgeoisie – preferred things produced by hand. Handmade products came to symbolise refinement and class. They were better finished, individually produced, and carefully designed. Machine-made goods were for export to the colonies. In countries with labour shortage, industrialists were keen on using mechanical power so that the need for human labour can be minimised. This was the case in nineteenth-century America. Britain, however, had no problem hiring human hands.

Answer the following MCQs by choosing the most appropriate option

37.1 When there is plenty of labour, wages are

    (a) Optimal   (b) Ideal   (c) High   (d)   Low

37.2 Why did the industrialists not want to introduce machines

    (a) Because of large investment   (b) Availability of plenty of labour

    (c) both a and b   (d) none of the above

37.3 At the waterfront, __________ was the time that ships were repaired and spruced up.

    (a) Summer   (b) Winter   (c) Spring (d)   Autumn

37.4 Consider the following statements:

    1.   Machines were oriented to producing goods with intricate designs and specific shapes

    2.   The demand in the market was often for uniforms, standardised goods.

    Which of the statement(s) given above is/are correct?

    (a) 1 only   (b) 2 only   (c) Both 1 and 2   (d)   Neither 1 nor 2

38. **Read the text given below and answer the following questions.**

Mass communication provides entertainment and creates awareness among people about various national programmes and policies. It includes radio, television, newspapers, magazines, books and films. All India Radio (Akashwani) broadcasts a variety of programmes in national, regional and local languages for various categories of people, spread over different parts of the country. Doordarshan, the national television channel of India, is one of the largest terrestrial networks in the world. It broadcasts a variety of programmes from entertainment, educational to sports, etc. for people of different age groups. India publishes a large number of newspapers and periodicals annually. They are of different types depending upon their periodicity. Newspapers are published in about 100 languages and dialects. Did you know that the largest number of newspapers published in the country are in Hindi, followed by English and Urdu? India is the largest producer of feature films in the world. It produces short films; video feature films and video short films. The Central Board of Film Certification is the authority to certify both Indian and foreign films.

Answer the following MCQs by choosing the most appropriate option

38.1 Mass communication provides among people

    (a) Newspapers   (b) Entertainment (c) Policies (d)   Programmes

38.2 Doordarshan, the national television channel of India, is one of the largest______ networks in the world.

   (a) News   (b) Arial   (c) Film   (d)   Terrestrial

38.3 Which of the following represent the correct descending order of languages in which largest number of newspapers published in the country?

   (a) English-Hindi-Urdu   (b) Urdu-English-Hindi

   (c) Hindi-Urdu-English   (d) Hindi-English-Urdu

38.4 Consider the following statements:

   1.   Newspapers are published in about 100 languages and dialects.

   2.   India is the largest producer of feature films in the world.

   Which of the statement(s) given above is/are correct?

   (a) 1 only   (b) 2 only   (c) Both 1 and 2   (d)   Neither 1 nor 2

39.   **Read the given extract and answer the following questions.**

Political parties need to face and overcome some challenges in order to remain effective instruments of democracy. The first challenge is lack of internal democracy within parties. All over the world there is a tendency in political parties towards the concentration of power in one or few leaders at the top. Parties do not keep membership registers, do not hold organisational meetings, and do not conduct internal elections regularly. Ordinary members of the party do not get sufficient information on what happens inside the party. They do not have the means or the connections needed to influence the decisions. As a result the leaders assume greater power to make decisions in the name of the party. Since one or few leaders exercise paramount power in the party, those who disagree with the leadership find it difficult to continue in the party. More than loyalty to party principles and policies, personal loyalty to the leader becomes more important. The second challenge of dynastic succession is related to the first one. Since most political parties do not practice open and transparent procedures for their functioning, there are very few ways for an ordinary worker to rise to the top in a party. Those who happen to be the leaders are in a position of unfair advantage to favour people close to them or even their family members. In many parties, the top positions are always controlled by members of one family. This is unfair to other members of that party. This is also bad for democracy, since people who do not have adequate experience or popular support come to occupy positions of power. This tendency is present in some measure all over the world, including in some of the older democracies.

Answer the following MCQs by choosing the most appropriate option

39.1 Which of the following is one of the challenges faced by the political parties?

   (a) Ample distribution of power   (b) Lack of internal democracy

   (c) Lack of funding   (d) None of the above

39.2 What is dynastic succession in the political parties?

    (a)   Periodic election

    (b)   Split in the party after few years

    (c)   Repeated succession to power by a few leaders

    (d)   A position of unfair advantage to the family members.

39.3 Why does personal loyalty to the leader becomes more important, more than loyalty to party principles and policies?

    (a)   Because of concentration of power in few hands

    (b)   Fear of losing membership

    (c)   Both a and b

    (d)   None of the above.

39.4 Consider the following statements:

    1.   Ordinary party members do not have the means or the connections needed to influence the decisions.

    2.   Ordinary members of the party do not get sufficient information on what happens inside the party.

    Which of the statement(s) given above is/are incorrect?

    (a) 1 only   (b) 2 only   (c) Both 1 and 2   (d)   Neither 1 nor 2

40. **Read the source given below and answer the following questions:**

Suppose for the present that a particular country is quite developed. We would certainly like this level of development to go up further or at least be maintained for future generations. This is obviously desirable. However, since the second half of the twentieth century, a number of scientists have been warning that the present type, and levels, of development are not sustainable. Groundwater is an example of renewable resources. These resources are replenished by nature as in the case of crops and plants. However, even these resources may be overused. For example, in the case of groundwater, if we use more than what is being replenished by rain then we would be overusing this resource. Non-renewable resources are those which will get exhausted after years of use. We have a fixed stock on earth which cannot be replenished. We do discover new resources that we did not know of earlier. New sources in this way add to the stock. However, over time, even this will get exhausted. Consequences of environmental degradation do not respect national or state boundaries; this issue is no longer region or nation specific. Our future is linked together. Sustainability of development is comparatively a new area of knowledge in which scientists, economists, philosophers and other social scientists are working together. In general, the question of development or progress is perennial. At all times as a member of society and as individuals we need to ask where we want to go, what we wish to become and what our goals are. So the debate on development continues.

Answer the following MCQs by choosing the most appropriate option

40.1 Since when a number of scientists been warning that the present type, and levels of development are not sustainable?

(a) Second half of the nineteenth century (b) Second half of the twentieth century

(c) First half of the twenty first century (d) Since the beginning

40.2 Groundwater is an example of _______________ resources.

(a) Perishable (b) Inexhaustible (c) Non-renewable (d) Renewable

40.3 The Consequences of environmental degradation are:

(a) Specific to every nation (b) Limited to national boundaries

(c) Limited to state boundaries (d) Not specific to nations

40.4 Consider the following statements:

1. We have a fixed stock on earth which cannot be replenished.

2. Sustainability of development is comparatively an old area of knowledge among scientists.

Which of the statement(s) given above is/are correct?

(a) 1 only (b) 2 only (c) Both 1 and 2 (d) Neither 1 nor 2

41. **Read the source given below and answer the questions that follows:**

Following the defeat of Napoleon in 1815, European governments were driven by a spirit of conservatism. Conservations believed that established, traditional institutions of state and society - like the monarchy, the Church, social hierarchies, property and the family-should be preserved. Most conservatives, however, did not propose a return to the society of pre-revolutionary days. Rather, they realised, from the changes initiated by Napoleon, that modernisation could in fact strangthen traditional institutions like the monarchy. It could make state power more effective and stronger. A modern army, an efficient bureaucracy, a dynamic economy, the absolition of feudalism and seridom could strangthen the autocratic monarchies of Europe in 1815, representatives of the European powers who had collectively defeated Napoleon, met at Viena to draw up a settlement for Europe. The Congress was hosted by the Austrian Chancellor Duke Metterntch. The delegates draw up the Treaty of Vienna of 1815 with the object of undoing most of the changes that had come about in Europe during the Napoleonic wars. The Bourbon dynasty, which had been deposed during the French Revolution, was restored to power, and France lost the terriories it had annexed under Napoleon. A series of states were set up on the boundaries of France to prevent French expansion in future.

Answer the following MCQs by choosing the most appropriate option.

41.1 European conservative ideology is best explained by

    (a)   Preservation of believes introduced by Napoleon

    (b)   Preservation of two sects of Christianity

    (c)   Preservation of socialist ideology in economic sphere

    (d)   Preservation of traditionalist beliefs in state and society

41.2 What was the purpose of the Vienna of Congress in 1815?

    (a)   To declare competition of German unification

    (b)   To restore conservative regime in Europe

    (c)   To declare war against France

    (d)   To start the process of Italian Unification

41.3. The conservatives focused on ______________ at the Congress of Vienna?

    (a)   To re-establish peace and stability in Europe

    (b)   To establish socialism in Europe

    (c)   To introduce democracy in France

    (d)   To set up a new Parliament in Austria

41.4 The Vienna Congress ensured peace in Europe by

    (a)   With the restoration of Bourbon Dynasty

    (b)   Austria was not given the control of Northern Italy

    (c)   Laying out a balance of power between all the great powers in Europe

    (d)   By giving power to the German confederation

42. **Read the text given below and answer the following questions:**

Manufacturing industries not only in modernising agriculture, which forms the backbone of our economy, they also reduce the heavy dependence of people on agricultural income by providing them jobs in secondary and tertiary sectors. Industrial development is a precondition for eradication of unemployment and poverty from our country. This was the main philosophy behind public sector industries and joint sector ventures in India. It was also aimed at bringing down regional disparties by establishing industries in tribal and backward areas. Export of manufactured goods expands trade and commerce, and brings in much needed foreign exchange. Countries that transform their raw materials into a wide variety of finished goods of higher vlaue are prosperous. India's prosperity lies in increasing and diversityfing its manufacturing industries as quickly as possible. Agriculture and industry are not exclusive of each other. They move hand in hand. For instance, the agro-insudtries in India have given a major boost to agriculture by raising its productivity.

42. Answer the following MCQs by choosing the most appropriate option.

42.1 Agriculture falls in ______________.

(a) Primary Sector

(b) Secondary Sector

(c) Tertiary Sector

(d) Quaternary Sector

42.2 Identify which sector the following jobs bleongs to-

Jobs created or promoted by manufacturing industries	Sector
a. Garment production	1. Primary
b. Research & Development	2. Tertiary
c. Banking	3. Secondary
d. Mining	4. Quaternary

Choose the correct option-

(a) a. 1, b. 2, c. 3, d. 4

(b) a. 3, b. 4, c. 2, d. 1

(c) a. 2, b. 3, c. 1, d. 2

(d) a. 4, b. 1, c. 4, d. 3

42.3 Which of the following options help in modernising agriculture?

(a) Manufacturing farm equipment

(b) all of these

(c) Supplying fertilizers and pestitides

(d) Producing tube well pumps and srinkelrs

42.4 Which of the following developments leads to attraction of foreign manufacturing firms?

(a) Agarian facilities

(b) Cultivable lands

(c) Media facilities

(d) Infrastructure facilities

43. **Read the given extract and answer the following quesitons.**

In a democracy, we are most concerned with ensuring that people will have the right to choose their rulers and people will have control over the rulers. Whenever possible and necessary, citizens should be able to participate in decision making, that affects them all. Therefore, the most basic outcome of democracy should be that if produces a government that is accountable to the citizerns, and responsive to the needs and expectations of the citizens. Some people think that democracy produces less effective government. It is, of course, true that non-democratic rulers are very quick and efficient in decision making and implementation, whereas, democracy is based on the idea of deliberation and negotation. So, some delay is bound to take place. But, because it has followed procedures, its decisions may be both more acceptable to the people and more effective. Moreover, when citizens want to know if a decision was taken through the correct procedures, they can find this out. They have the right and the means to examine the process of decision making. this is known as transparency. This factor is often missing from a non-democratic government. There is another aspect in which democratic government is certainly better than its alternatives: democratic government is legitimate government. It may be slow, less efficient, not always very responsive of clean. But a democratic government is people's own government.

43. **Answer the following MCQs by choosing the most appropriate option**

43.1 People's right to choose their rulers is best described as the-

    (a) Right to Initiate   (b) Right to Plebiscite

    (c) Right to Vote   (d) Right to Referendum

43.2 For promoting transparency in the governance, which of the following will help?

    (a) Right to education   (b) Right to information

    (c) Right against exploitation   (d) Right to speech and expression

43.3 The legitimacy of the government is marked by

    (a) Credibility of politicians   (b) People's movements

    (c) Free and fair elections   (d) Holding of powers

43.4 Decisions in a democracy are more acceptable to the people if they are-

    (a) Taken swiftly and implemented quickly

    (b) Taken by giving privileges to the people

    (c) Taken through elites' votes

    (d) Taken after following due processes

44. **Read the source given below and answer the following questions:**

Ford Motors, an American company, is one of the world's largest automobile manufacturers with production spread over 26 countries of the world. Ford Motors came to India in 1995 and spent ₹ 1700 crore to set up a large plant near Chennai. This was done in collaboration with Mahindra and Mahindra, a major Indian manufacturer of jeeps and trucks. By the year 2004. Ford Motors was selling 27.000 cars in the Indian markets, while 24.000 cars were exporter from India to South Aftica, Mexico and Brazil. The company wanted to develop Ford India as a component supplying base for its other plants across the globe.

Answer the following MCQs by choosing the most appropriate option

44.1 Which of the following options relates to the above passage?

    (a) Increased employment   (b) Foreign investment

    (c) Foreign collaboration   (d) International competition

44.2 By setting up their production plants in India, Ford Motors wishes to –

    (a) Collaborate with a leading Indian Automobile company

    (b) Satisfy the demands of American, African and Indian markets

    (c) Tap the benefits of low-cost production and a large market

    (d) Take over small automobile manufacturing units in India

44.3 Ford Motors can be termed as a Multi-National Company based on?

    (a) Production of different types of automobiles

    (b) Largest automobile manufacturer in the world

    (c) Because of largescale exports of cars across globe

    (d) Industrial and commertial ventures across globe

44.4 Ford Motors' wish to develop Ford India as a component supplying base is an example of-

    (a) Promoting local industries of India   (b) Merging trade from different countries

    (c) Supplying jobs to factors workers in India   (d) Interlinking of production across countries

Case Study Based MCQs
Solution

1.1. (d)	**1.2.** (b)	**1.3.** (a)	**1.4.** (c)
2.1. (d)	**2.2.** (b)	**2.3.** (b)	**2.4.** (d)
3.1. (c)	**3.2.** (b)	**3.3.** (c)	**3.4.** (d)
4.1. (b)	**4.2.** (d)	**4.3.** (c)	**4.4.** (d)
5.1. (d)	**5.2.** (d)	**5.3.** (c)	**5.4.** (b)
6.1. (c)	**6.2.** (b)	**6.3.** (b)	**6.4.** (a)
7.1. (a)	**7.2.** (d)	**7.3.** (c)	**7.4.** (c)
8.1. (a)	**8.2.** (d)	**8.3.** (a)	**8.4.** (a)
9.1 (d)	**9.2** (b)	**9.3** (b)	**9.4** (c)
10.1 (d)	**10.2** (c)	**10.3** (d)	**10.4** (d)
11.1 (c)	**11.2** (b)	**11.3** (b)	**11.4** (a)
12.1 (c)	**12.2** (d)	**12.3** (b)	**12.4** (d)
13.1 (d)	**13.2** (d)	**13.3** (d)	**13.4** (a)
14.1 (b)	**14.2** (d)	**14.3** (a)	**14.4** (d)
15.1 (a)	**15.2** (d)	**15.3** (a)	**15.4** (d)
16.1 (a)	**16.2** (d)	**16.3** (b)	**16.4** (c)
17.1 (b)	**17.2** (c)	**17.3** (b)	**17.4** (d)
18.1 (c)	**18.2** (d)	**18.3** (d)	**18.4** (d)
19.1 (c)	**19.2** (b)	**19.3** (d)	**19.4** (d)
20.1 (b)	**20.2** (d)	**20.3** (a)	**20.4** (c)
21.1 (c)	**21.2** (d)	**21.3** (a)	**21.4** (b)
22.1 (d)	**22.2** (d)	**22.3** (d)	**22.4** (a)
23.1 (d)	**23.2** (c)	**23.3** (a)	**23.4** (d)
24.1 (b)	**24.2** (d)	**24.3** (d)	**24.4** (c)
25.1 (d)	**25.2** (c)	**25.3** (d)	**25.4** (a)
26.1 (a)	**26.2** (d)	**26.3** (c)	**26.4** (d)
27.1 (d)	**27.2** (d)	**27.3** (a)	**27.4** (b)
28.1 (c)	**28.2.** (d)	**28.3** (d)	**28.4** (b)

29.1 (d)	**29.2**	(b)	**29.3**	(d)	**29.4**	(b)
30.1 (c)	**30.2**	(c)	**30.3**	(a)	**30.4**	(a)
31.1 (b)	**31.2**	(c)	**31.3**	(c)	**31.4**	(a)
32.1 (c)	**32.2**	(d)	**32.3**	(d)	**32.4**	(d)
33.1. (d)	**33.2.**	(d)	**33.3.**	(d)	**33.4.**	(c)
34.1. (b)	**34.2.**	(d)	**34.3.**	(d)	**34.4.**	(a)
35.1. (b)	**35.2.**	(d)	**35.3.**	(a)	**35.4.**	(b)
36.1. (c)	**36.2.**	(a)	**36.3.**	(b)	**36.4.**	(c)
37.1. (d)	**37.2.**	(c)	**37.3.**	(b)	**37.4.**	(d)
38.1. (b)	**38.2.**	(d)	**38.3.**	(d)	**38.4.**	(c)
39.1. (b)	**39.2.**	(d)	**39.3.**	(c)	**39.4.**	(d)
40.1. (b)	**40.2.**	(d)	**40.3.**	(d)	**40.4.**	(a)
41.1 (d)	**41.2**	(b)	**41.3**	(a)	**41.4**	(c)
42.1 (d)	**42.2**	(b)	**42.3**	(b)	**42.4**	(d)
43.1 (c)	**43.2**	(b)	**43.3**	(c)	**43.4**	(d)
44.1 (b)	**44.2**	(c)	**44.3**	(d)	**44.4**	(d)